Pat!
Thanks so
much!
Wow... go Cork!

Love,
Susan
1·16·20

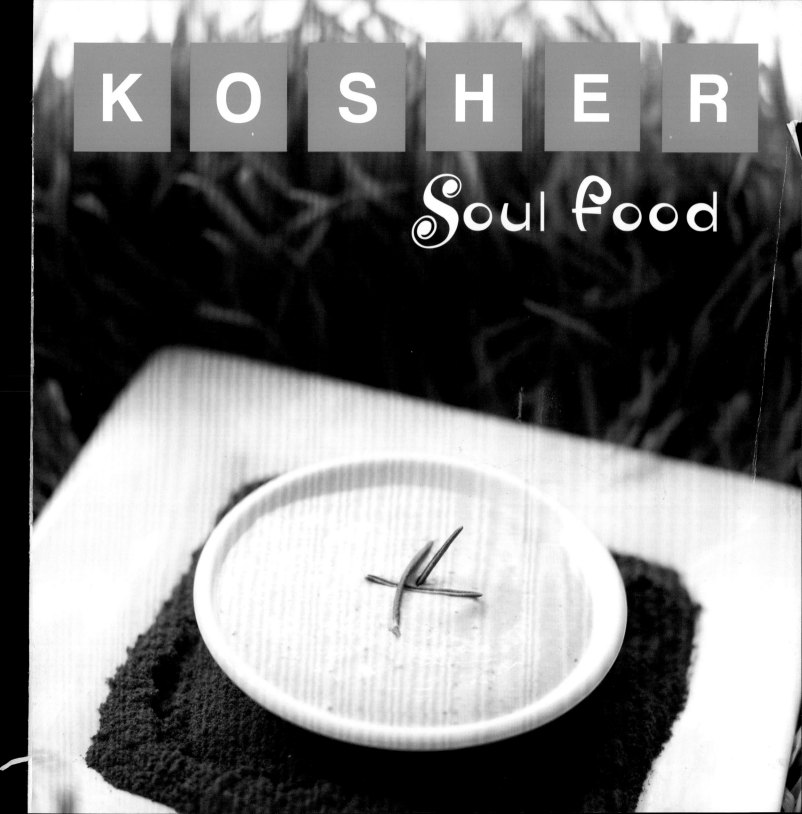

KOSHER
Soul Food

KOSHER

Soul food

a cookbook by

Sunda Croonquist

with **Chef Nir**

Putnam & Smith Publishing Co.

Los Angeles

First Published in 2015 by Putnam & Smith Publishing Company, a division of Putnam & Smith

ISBN 978-1-939986-01-6

Library of Congress Control Number: 2014951875

Book, Jacket, and Case Photography by Antonio Busiello
Book, Jacket, and Case Design by William Reynolds with David Pascal
Food Styling by Rita Miscioscia
Editing by Sue Katz

Printed in China

I dedicate this book to my grandmother Eva Mae Brown who taught me the beauty of Soul Food and to my mother-in-law Ruth Zafrin who taught me that "everyone can eat Kosher but not everyone can eat Non-Kosher!"

I also want to dedicate this book to my parents Sandra and Harold Croonquist without them there would be no Sunda!

Headlining this dedication is my dear husband Mark Zafrin who has his own special recipe of love and encouragement also known as Aviva and Tovah, our daughters. I dedicate this book to you all.

Contents

Foreword

Sunda is one of Hollywood's best-kept secrets and most talented and diverse stars. I have had some of Sunda's Kosher Soul Food at her Passover dinners. I have to tell you I have been around some of the most famous chefs in Hollywood and I have never had a Passover dinner where I have finished my plate and asked for seconds...except at Sunda's. Her meals come with a healthy portion of laughter. I'm sure you will laugh and cook some of your best meals using Sunda's book. If you come to the Laugh Factory and show me a copy of the book I will personally send you a pair of tickets to come back. Make sure you get her autograph on this book, it will be worth plenty!

Jamie Masada

Founder and President of Laugh Factory

Special Thanks. I Know It's a Lot But You're All Worth The Ink!

To my husband Mark Zafrin for his love and support and never complaining about a meal! Coffee yes, brisket no!

To my beautiful daughters who always want two separate meals and made me a speed cook! Aviva and Tovah, you are my world!

To Sue and George Shouldis for making this decade of a dream a reality and they thanked me for all of the sleepless nights!

To my little brother Jamar, for being my taste tester in my early years even when I baked clear wrap into the mac and cheese…oops!

To my aunts and uncle (The kids of Eva Brown!). Thanks for helping me out as a kid. I didn't forget and I'm hoping you don't remember!

To my sister Linda Sue and Cousin Faye Lynn who understand how frustrating it is to spell out CROONQUIST and have Southern names that better help sell this book! Cousin Joanne counts but she changed her last name to Fusco! THAT'S SO JERSEY!

To my Croonquist "Clan" from Florida, Donald, Tommy, & Kelly, I would love to scuba dive with you but I just can't get my hair wet!

To James Harris my comedy partner, for always "volunteering" to help me in the kitchen…when I hold up a knife!

To the Weinblut family. I thank you for sharing your son, father and husband for this book. Who knew that there were actual measurements for cooking?

To Mika Hamado-Ano for always entertaining the kids while I cook and teaching them how to download apps!

To Jamie Masada for always making me work at The World Famous Laugh Factory when my feet hurt after a long day of cooking!

To my dear friend Susan Hall for laughing with me while she watched me cook for parties which I made believe were catered. (They never knew!)

To my nieces Ashanti, Karen, Amara, Jackie and Leanne…I know, I don't bake enough for you!

To Uncle Joe Croonquist and Aunt Val, I thank you from the bottom of my heart for loving me for who I am.

To my Weaver kin from Georgia! You know who you are! This book is possible because our great grandmother Nancy taught our "Big Mommas" how to cook. Our husbands are grateful… and it shows!

To Phil Blazer, Jon McCandless and all my friends from Jewish Life Television, thank you for my talk show! You are the Chosen Network!

To Aishia Deal, Danielle Smith, Erika Gonzales for helping me with the book, Bat Mitzvah, and craziness!

Special thanks to NY Publicist Gordon Balkcom who 10 years ago advertised this book before it became a book!

To NJ's "The Record" newspaper thank you for keeping me in print.

To Karen Gilbert-Hansford for believing in me when no one else did! But can you blame them!

To my friends from Sinai Temple in LA, my DADA moms from The Debbie Allen Dance Academy and all my friends, especially New Jersey, who had to bear the burden of constantly hearing me say, "I'm writing a cookbook! I can't talk!"

Rabbi Chaim Mentz of Chabad of Bel Air, who prayed for me while I was writing the book and the Rebbetson, his wife, Charna who was gracious and invited us for so many great Shabbat dinners with his family, which gave me a much needed break!

To Ali Hosseinpour from Fab of L.A., for the use of their props in our photo shoot.

My family and friends from Paterson, New Jersey, I love you all and know that I'm still Jersey Strong!

And a Special Word From Our Chef

First, I would like to thank Sunda for bringing me into her dream of this book.

To my wife, Tere, who has supported and believed in me from the very beginning. She has stood by me every step of the way. Honey, none of this would have happened without you.

To my great kids, Jacob, Tani, Michelle & Daniel, who have always supported me and were always my toughest critics.

To my Mom, who saw my dream and knew I could achieve it. You taught me everything I know and made me shine. You are always thinking of me.

To my amazing staff, thank you for making it happen on a daily basis.

And a big Thank You to my friends and clients who have supported us for many years and still make every day worth it all.

Food

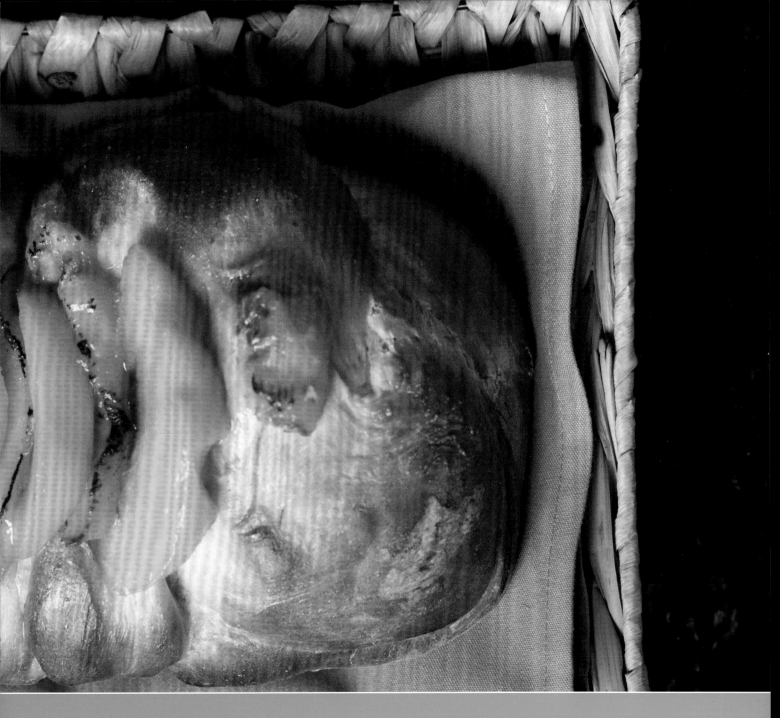

brings the World together

What is Soul Food? To quote the author Bob Jeffries in his 1969 "Soul Food Cookbook": "While all soul food is southern food, not all southern food is Soul. Soul Food cooking is an example of how a really good southern Negro cooked with what they had available to them." For me, Soul Food was my Grandma Eva's Cooking!

I grew up in Paterson, New Jersey to a Swedish father and Black mother. My mother's parents were from Decatur, Georgia. As a "Jersey Girl" with this unique fusion of cultures, I learned to combine my worlds with recipes and ingredients of my multi-cultural heritage. The Kosher Soul Food cookbook is a guide for integrating two very different culinary worlds. I was heavily influenced on my mother's side of the family because that cooking was just so good and the stories that go along with these recipes provide a lot of my childhood "soul" experiences that I have used as fodder for my stand up comedy!

My grandfather Abraham loved bluefish. My mouth still waters when I think of bluefish broiling in my grandma's oven and the time Grandpa Abe left fresh cooked bluefish on the table and turned his back for a moment too long as Tigger the cat had run off with it! You can't blame that cat...it was good!

I lived a sheltered life as a child. I attended a Catholic school where there weren't many African Americans and certainly not much of food like Grandma Eva's. When my friends came to my house, they loved her cooking. Some of my Black friends also had "Soul Food" in their homes but it was very different than Grandma Eva's. It was mostly "hog maws and chittlin's!" Hog maws were pig's stomachs and chitterlings aka "chitlin's" were pig's intestines and they smelled sooo bad! I once told my friend Starlet that something died in her house because I could smell it! She corrected me, "That's dinner!" I was mortified. This is the kind of soul food that never made it to my grandmother's table.

As I grew older I remember when my mom's little brother "Uncle Junie" became involved in the Black Power Movement. "Dashikis" replaced undershirts, and some young Black men and women embraced the "Natural" look, letting their hair grow out into Afros and referred to themselves as "Brothers" and "Sisters." That was the 70's. I have to stop dating myself! But if I don't, who will? That's a joke. What isn't a joke is that my Grandma's cooking took a political turn out of nowhere for me. For the first time, my Grandma Eva's cooking was referred to as "soul food"

To those who wonder why I wanted to write this book once you taste these recipes you will know! Now you have learned a little something about what is Kosher and what is Soul Food. You will also learn a little something about a funny Jersey Girl with a funny name. This book is dedicated to the people in my life who love to eat and love to laugh! This book is for YOU!

L'CHAIM!

What is **Kosher?** "Man does not live by bread alone" is a famous saying that we all know, but it actually comes from the Bible and refers to the Manna that came from the heavens when the Jewish people came out of Egypt. This is a reminder to us that what we eat comes from G-D and this is why we obey the Biblical Kosher laws..

The Basic Rules for keeping a Kosher kitchen:

Meat and dairy products are not allowed to be cooked, prepared or eaten together. China, flatware and utensils for preparing, storing, and eating are all kept separate and washed separately.

Kosher meat is slaughtered in a special way. A Shochet is a highly trained Rabbi who slaughters the animal by hand according to Jewish Law. The Kosher slaughtering is considered the most efficient, cleanest and least painful way to slaughter the animal. The animal is examined to ensure it is healthy. There may be no broken bones, holes in the lungs and the animal must be in the healthiest condition. There are no exceptions.

The Kosher part of a cow is only its front quarter. To remove any blood which is not Kosher, the meat has to be salted and soaked using Kosher salt. This is how kosher salt got its name. After a period of time, the salt is washed off.

Parve. Foods like rice, vegetables and potatoes are called Parve. These products are neither meat nor dairy. To stay Parve, they're prepared in utensils that must remain Parve and are never used for meat or dairy.

Eggs are fine. We just need to check for any blood spots. Any eggs with any blood spots must be discarded.

Fish with fins and scales are Kosher and can be eaten cooked or raw. Fish need no special Koshering process but they cannot be mixed with chicken or meat. All other seafood is not Kosher, and is forbidden.

All food products that are processed must have a Kosher certification on them. This includes juices, cheese, condiments, and canned goods.

Fresh vegetables must be washed thoroughly and checked for insects. That extra protein is not Kosher!

Passover Kosher Laws. These are even stricter than basic Kosher laws. Just a note, if you receive an invite to dinner on Passover, accept it. But do not take any food products to a friend's house on Passover that are not certified Kosher for Passover, or you will never be invited again. Talk about the Matzo hitting the fan!!!

Rules and Laws of the Sabbath. The Sabbath, also known as "Shabbat", starts at sunset Friday evening, and ends sundown on Saturday night. There are many restrictions during that time including the use of electricity in any form or fashion, and cooking or using an open fire. Any foods that will be used for Friday night dinner must be on the fire or in the oven before the Sabbath starts.

To bring in the Sabbath - referred to as "The Sabbath Queen" - the woman of the house lights the Sabbath candles that represents the creation of the world. The husband then says a prayer to glorify the lady of the house, and blesses his children. We then go into the Friday night Kiddush service where we bless the Sabbath with wine and the Challah. We all sit and partake in this great dinner which is a moment for your body, mind and soul.

STOCKS
& RUBS

Roux

1 cup unsalted margarine
1 1/2 cups of flour

Heat the margarine over a medium-high heat. Add flour all at once while whisking vigorously. Reduce heat to medium and continue whisking less vigorously. Cook until mixture becomes light almond in color and you smell a nice aroma.

You can store roux for up to 4 weeks in an airtight container.

Nir's Tip: When thickening a liquid, make sure you bring liquid to a boil and crumble roux into small pieces so there are fewer clumps in the liquid, and constantly mix while boiling.

Vegetable Stock

Makes 10-12 cups

16 cups of water plus 2 more cups for deglazing
2 tbsp canola oil
1 large onion peeled and sliced thin
1 sliced carrot
3 stalks of celery
1 whole tomato
1 cup sliced mushrooms
1 tsp kosher salt
1 tsp pepper
4 garlic cloves
3 bay leaves

Preheat a large pot and add oil. Once hot, add the onion and sauté until soft and golden. Add carrots, mushrooms and celery and continue to sauté until vegetables begin to caramelize.

Add 2 cups of water and deglaze the bottom of pot. Add remainder of water. Add salt, pepper, tomato, garlic and bay leaves and bring to a boil. Reduce the heat and simmer for 60-90 minutes.

Nir's Tip: For a thicker stock, add a cup of small cubed potatoes as it will add a little body to the stock

this is "Fur" my Vegan Homies

Veal Stock

Makes 10-12 cups

10 meaty veal bones
5 tbsp canola oil
1 1/2 tbsp tomato paste
5 carrots cut into thirds
6 celery stalks cut into thirds and washed well
3 unpeeled onions cut into quarters
1 whole unpeeled garlic head
5 sprigs of fresh thyme
2 sprigs of fresh sage
5 dry bay leaves
16 cups of water plus 2 cups of water for deglazing
1 tsp of kosher salt
1 tbsp of whole black peppercorns

Preheat the oven to 450°F.

In a large roasting pan, arrange veal bones, oil them evenly and season with salt and pepper. Roast bones in oven flipping them after 20-30 minutes. Roast for 50-60 minutes longer. Remove from oven when bones are a golden brown.

Place carrots, celery, onion, leeks and garlic around the bones. Smear tomato paste over bones. Return to oven and roast for 45-60 minutes.

Into a large stockpot add roasted bones, roasted vegetables, tomato paste, thyme, rosemary, sage and 16 cups of water. Discard fat from the roasting pan. Place roasting pan directly onto stovetop and heat on medium for 1 minute. Add 2 cups of water to roasting pan while scraping up brown bits on the bottom of pan. Add deglazed liquid to stockpot. Bring liquid to a boil and simmer for 7-8 hours, skimming and discarding froth frequently.

Once reduced to 5 cups, pour the stock through a large sieve and press the vegetables with a ladle to get all juices out.

Discard solids that remain and let stock cool. If you are going to use immediately, skim fat off top after letting sit for five minutes. If you plan to store the stock, place in a refrigerator overnight.

The next day there will be a layer of fat on top. Remove fat. The remainder of the stock can be covered, refrigerated and stored for up to a week. You can also divide stock into smaller containers and freeze for up to 3 months.

Nir's Tip: By letting the fat settle on the top of the stock while it cools, it also protects the stock from bacteria entering the liquid and containers lengthening the life of the stock. After all those hours of work, it's worth it!

Beef Stock

Makes 10-12 cups

4-5 lbs short ribs or meaty beef shanks
5 tbsp canola oil
5 carrots cut into thirds
6 celery stalks cut into thirds and washed well
3 unpeeled onions cut into quarters
1 whole unpeeled garlic head
5 sprigs of fresh thyme
5 sprigs of fresh sage
3 sprigs of fresh rosemary
5 bay leaves
16 cups of water plus 2 cups of water for deglazing
1 tsp of kosher salt
1 tbsp of whole black peppercorns

Preheat the oven to 450°F.

In a large roasting pan, arrange short ribs or beef shanks, oil them evenly and season with salt and pepper. Roast for 50-60 minutes. Remove from oven when bones are a golden brown. Don't worry if they are a little crispy or crunchy.

Add carrots, celery, onion, leeks, and garlic around the bones. Return to oven and roast for 45-60 minutes.

Into a large stockpot, add roasted bones, roasted vegetables, thyme, rosemary, sage and 16 cups of water. Discard fat from roasting pan.

Place roasting pan directly onto stovetop and heat on medium for 1 minute. Add 2 cups of water to roasting pan while scraping up brown bits on the bottom of pan. Add deglazed liquid to stockpot. Bring liquid to a boil and simmer for 7-8 hours, skimming and discarding the froth frequently.

Once reduced to 5-6 cups, pour stock through a large sieve and press vegetables to get all the juices from the overcooked vegetables. Discard the vegetables that remain and cool stock. If you are using immediately, let stock sit for five minutes, and then skim off fat from top. If you are storing the stock, place in a refrigerator overnight. The next day, there will be a layer of congealed fat on top. Remove and then you can refrigerate it for up to a week, or divide into smaller containers and you can keep in freezer for up to 3 months.

Nir's Tip: When buying short ribs for ribs or even back ribs, or oxtails, you can save the fatty ribs or bones with not much meat for the stock - the ones people may not want to eat. You can use any kind of meaty beef bone for stock and store in the freezer for future use.

Chicken Stock

Makes 10-12 cups

5 3/4 lbs of chicken pieces
16 cups of water
1 large unpeeled onion cut in half
6 stalks of celery washed and cut into thirds
5 large carrots washed and cut into fourths
2 bay leaves
1 tbsp whole black peppercorns

Place chicken and water in a large pot over a high heat. Add onions, celery, carrots, bay leaves and whole peppercorns.

Bring liquid to a boil and add remaining 2 cups of water. Reduce heat and simmer for 3-4 hours. Skim top as needed.

Remove chicken and let cool. Remove vegetables and discard. Pour stock through a sieve and let cool. If storing stock, place in a refrigerator overnight. The next day, there will be a layer of fat on top. Remove and refrigerate in a covered container for up to a week.

You can also divide stock into smaller containers. This can be frozen in an airtight container for up to 3 months.

Nir's Tip: Do not add salt. Kosher poultry is already salted for Koshering. Add later to taste when making soups, sauces and gravies. The chicken meat from the soup can be used to top salads, make a great chicken salad or even a chicken sandwich. You can also freeze and store for later use.

Ground Garlic

Makes 3/4 cup

1/2 cup whole garlic peeled
1/4 cup olive oil or canola oil

Place garlic and oil in food processor. Pulse a few times or let run 20-30 seconds until as smooth as you like. Refrigerate in an airtight container, and start to cook. Garlic makes the difference in the flavor of the food.

Nir's Tip: This should be a staple in every kitchen. Today, you have the convenience of buying whole peeled garlic everywhere.

At least we can be sure that Vampires won't be sitting at my table!

Cajun Mix

Makes 3/4 cup

2 tsp basil powder
2 tsp dry rosemary powder
2 tsp garlic powder
2 tsp granulated garlic
2 tsp kosher salt
2 tsp mustard seeds
3 tsp thyme
4 tsp cayenne pepper
4 tsp ground black pepper
4 tsp onion powder
4 tsp paprika
4 tsp white pepper

Place all ingredients in a dry food processor and mix for 2-3 minutes. Mix and place in an airtight container. It may be stored for a few weeks if in a dry area.

Nir's Tip: Great for blackened chicken or for sautéing fish.

Cajun Spread

Makes 1 1/2 cups

1/4 cup of Cajun mix
1 lb margarine

Let margarine come to room temperature. Dice margarine into cubes and place in a mixer. Add Cajun mix slowly and increase speed until mixture is whipped. Remove and refrigerate in an airtight container.

Nir's Tip: This spread can be used on bread alone, to sauté beef, chicken, fish, or even vegetables. It is a nice way to give a quick flavoring for a fast meal.

Cajun Mix...
this is what they call me in New Orleans!

STARTERS & SIDES

Crispy Chicken Drumettes with Peach and Ginger Marmalade

Serves 10 - 12

Drumettes

3 cups all-purpose flour
2 tbsp garlic powder
1 tbsp ground black pepper
1/2 tsp ground black pepper
1 tbsp paprika
1/2 tsp white pepper
2 tbsp onion powder
1 1/2 cups all-purpose flour
1 tsp kosher salt
1/4 cup mayonnaise
2 egg yolks, beaten
12 oz beer (may replace with water)
vegetable oil for frying
2 1/2 - 3 lbs of chicken drumettes (46 - 60 pieces)

In a large bowl, mix 3 cups flour, garlic powder, 1 tbsp black pepper, paprika, white pepper and onion powder.

In a separate bowl, mix 1 1/2 cups flour, 1 tsp salt, 1/2 tsp black pepper, egg yolks, mayonnaise and beer. You may need to thin with additional beer/water if the batter is too thick. Dip the drumettes in dry mix first then dip in wet batter and then cover and refrigerate for 30-45 minutes.

Using a heavy saucepan with a thick bottom, make sure to fill it at least 1/3 full with oil and heat to 350°F, using a thermometer. For extra crunch, you can take drumettes from wet batter and re-dip in the dry batter and place carefully in hot oil. Depending upon the size of the drumettes, it should take 6-8 minutes to cook thoroughly. Do not cook more that 5-6 drumettes at a time.

Remove from oil and place on paper towel.

Nir's Tip: If you do not have a deep fryer, and are using a pan, a thicker pan retains the heat better and helps the oil stay at the correct temperature for a better crunch. Also you may take the drummets from the refrigerator and let sit for 15-20 minutes on the counter while the oil heats up so the drummets are not cold. They will cook faster and evenly.

Peach and Ginger Marmalade Dipping Sauce

1 tbsp canola
1 large shallot diced
1 cup peach preserves
2 tbsp honey
2 tsp seasoned rice vinegar
1 tbsp ground fresh ginger
1 tbsp soy sauce
2 tbsp cold water

Heat saucepan with oil. Add shallot and sauté until it gets a golden color. Add rest of ingredients in saucepan and heat, stirring constantly. Bring to a boil and remove from heat immediately.

Nir's Tip: You can always add some chopped fresh peaches to your recipe when in season. Just cut up and add to the saucepan when you are mixing recipe. Put on a lower heat so the peaches get soft.

So simple to make, they should be called "Dumbettes!"

Candied Yam Chips

Serves 6 - 8

2 lbs sweet potatoes, washed & peeled
non-stick cooking spray
2 tsp granulated sugar
1/2 tsp onion powder
1/2 tsp kosher salt
1/8 tsp ground black pepper

Preheat oven to 350°F.

Cut each sweet potato widthwise into thin round slices. Place circle-cut sweet potatoes on oiled baking sheet. Bake 10-12 minutes. Make sure chips do not get brown. Remove from oven.

Spray sweet potatoes with oil. Mix sugar, salt, pepper and onion powder in a bowl. Sprinkle on potatoes evenly and roast another 8- 10 minutes until golden brown, turning over halfway through.

Candied Pastrami Strips

Serves 3 - 4

8 oz fatty pastrami sliced thin
1/2 cup brown sugar
spray oil

Preheat oven to 450°F.

Spray a cookie sheet pan with oil. Place pastrami strips on an oiled sheet pan. Pat brown sugar all over pastrami.

Place in oven for 6-8 minutes. Once sugar melts and creates a nice glaze remove from oven.

Remove strips from pan onto a plate or parchment paper. Let cool and serve.

Don't take this literally Candied Pastrami Strips will keep their clothes On!

Sunda's Sliders with Pulled Beef

Serves 4 - 5

Lamb & Beef Sliders

1 lb ground beef
1 lb ground lamb
1 tbsp chopped fresh Italian parsley
1 tsp chopped fresh dill
4 tsp chopped garlic
1 tsp kosher salt
1 tsp white pepper
1 1/2 tsp cumin

Mix all ingredients in a cold mixing bowl until they are properly mixed together. Make 12 even portions 1/2 inch thick. Place on a sheet pan and refrigerate for 1 hour. Cook on a preheated grill to medium well.

Pulled Beef

3-4 lbs of fatty brisket
1 tsp kosher salt
1 tsp freshly ground black pepper
3 tbsp canola oil
2 red onions cut in 1/2 inch slices
2 carrots cut into quarters
3 ribs celery cut into quarters
1 tbsp fresh garlic
2 cups of red wine
1 tsp onion powder
1 tsp fresh thyme
5 cups veal stock
3 tbsp tomato paste

Rub the brisket with salt, pepper, onion powder, fresh garlic and thyme. Heat oil in a large skillet and sear the meat on both sides. Place vegetables on the bottom of a large roasting pan. Remove the seared brisket and place over the vegetables. Pour wine over the meat. Add 3 cups veal stock to the roasting pan. Cover pan and place in preheated oven at 350°F. Roast for 3 1/2-4 hours.

Once meat is tender, remove from the roasting pan and pull brisket apart with a fork or your hands.

When brisket is completely pulled apart, take the liquid and vegetables and pour into a large blender or food processor. Purée until fine. With the remaining 2 cups of veal stock, dilute tomato paste and add to puréed liquid. Heat a large skillet and add liquid and pulled beef. Bring to a boil, reduce heat and simmer for 45 minutes.

Nir's Tip: For extra spice add cayenne pepper to the pulled beef.

Mini Slider Buns

Makes 24 buns

1 cup warm water
2 tbsp margarine
1 tbsp melted margarine
1 large egg
3 1/2 cups unbleached all-purpose flour
1/4 cup sugar
1/4 tsp kosher salt
1 tbsp instant yeast
1 tbsp poppy or sesame seeds

Preheat oven 375 degree°F.

Add water, sugar and yeast into a mixer and blend. Add rest of the ingredients. Knead dough until it is soft and smooth. Make sure dough does not stick to the side of mixing bowl. Remove dough from the mixer and cover. Let it rise for 1-2 hours or until doubled in size.

Gently deflate the dough and divide it into 24 even pieces. Shape each piece into a round ball and place on a lightly greased baking sheet. Flatten buns with your hand. Cover buns and let rise for another 45-60 minutes. Brush buns with melted margarine and sprinkle with poppy or sesame seeds. Bake 12-16 minutes until golden brown. Remove from oven and let cool.

Aunt Rose's Sweet Potato Fries with Spicy Ketchup

Serves 4 - 6

4 lbs orange sweet potatoes, peeled, long-cut
4 tbsp Cajun mix
2 tsp kosher salt
6 tbsp vegetable oil
1 tbsp ground garlic
black pepper, freshly ground to taste
1/2 cup chives

Place the sweet potatoes in large pot and cover with cold water. Bring to a boil and cook until slightly tender. Do not overcook. Drain potatoes well and let cool.

In a large bowl, add oil, spices and garlic and toss with the sweet potatoes. Heat a large skillet and add olive oil. Once hot add the potatoes and sauté. Let cook for a few minutes and then gently mix without breaking them. Continue to cook to a golden brown. Garnish with chives.

Spicy Ketchup

1 cup ketchup
1 tbsp Worcestershire sauce
1 tsp molasses
1 tsp fresh ground garlic
1 tsp cayenne pepper

Mix ingredients and serve with sweet potato fries.

Uncle Junie's New Years Eve Black Eyed Peas

Serves 4 - 6

1 (16-oz) package dried black-eyed peas
8 oz fatty pastrami
2 red peppers chopped small
1 can (16 oz) sweet corn
1 large red onion, chopped
1/2 tsp ground pepper
1 jalapeño pepper, seeded and diced
1 tbsp chopped green onions
1 tbsp crispy pastrami (recipe on page 76)
1 qt water

Pre-soak washed peas for 6-8 hours.

In a large pot, bring water to boil and add black eyed peas. While peas are boiling, heat a skillet and cook the fatty pastrami until fat starts to curl and melt. Add the peppers, chopped onions and sauté.

Cook peas covered for 1 hour. Check for tenderness. You do not want them too soft. Add the sauté mixture and drained corn. Cook until water evaporates, 45 minutes-1 hour.

Black eyed peas should not have too much liquid. Add green onions and chopped pastrami to garnish.

In southern homes making
Black Eyed Peas on
New Year's Day is a tradition
to bring money for the New Year.
I'm still waiting!

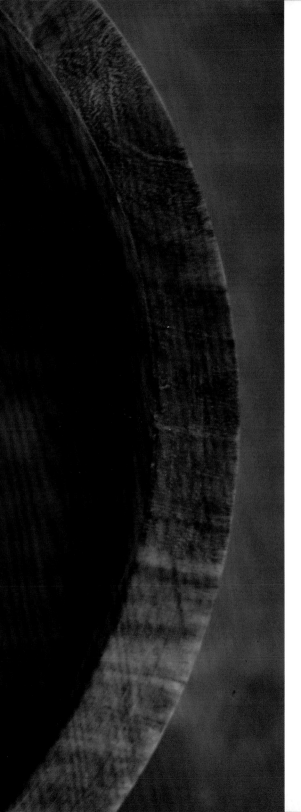

Home Fries

Serves 4 - 6

3 lbs boiled potatoes, chilled
6 tbsp canola oil
1 small yellow onion, diced
2 red peppers, diced
4 tbsp paprika
1/4 cup chopped Italian parsley
1/4 cup greens onions chopped
4 tbsp Cajun spice blend
kosher salt and freshly ground black pepper to taste

Cut chilled boiled potatoes into 1/2 inch cubes. For a rustic look and taste you can leave the skin on.

Heat a large skillet. While heating, mix potatoes, oil and spices; add onions and peppers and sauté until soft. Add seasoned potatoes and sauté. Let sit for a few minutes so potatoes get a crust on the bottom.

With a spatula, scrape from bottom to top, mixing potatoes until golden brown. Sprinkle top with parsley and green onion.

Nir's Tip: You may add diced pastrami or jalapeños.

Collard Greens with Crispy Pastrami

Serves 4 - 6

2 tbsp olive oil
6 slices beef pastrami, chopped small
1 large onion, chopped
1 tsp ground garlic
1 tsp kosher salt
1 tsp pepper
3 cups chicken stock or beef stock
1 pinch red pepper flakes
1 lb bag of chopped collard greens

Preheat a deep skillet or pot on medium heat. Add olive oil and chopped pastrami. Sauté until pastrami is crispy. Add onions and cook until tender. Add chili pepper and garlic, cook for one more minute. Add collard greens and sauté until they wilt.

Pour in the stock and cook for a few minutes. Reduce heat and cover. Let cook for 35-45 minutes, add the salt and pepper. Make sure collard greens are nice and tender.

Nothing is more Soulful than collard greens add some pastrami and you got Kosher Soul, Baby!

Aunt Lois' Red Rice

Serves 4 - 6

2 Spanish onions, minced
1/4 cup margarine
3 bay leaves
1 tbsp paprika
1 medium diced onion
1 red pepper diced small
1 tbsp chopped thyme
1 tbsp chopped basil
1 tbsp chopped marjoram
1 tbsp chopped sage
1/2 kosher salt
1/2 tsp black pepper
1 tsp onion powder
1 tsp garlic powder
1/2 cup tomato paste
1 cup long-grain rice
2 cups chicken or vegetable stock

In a separate pot melt margarine over medium heat. Once hot, add onions and peppers and sauté until soft. Add rice and sauté for a few more minutes. Add herbs, tomato paste, spices and stock. Mix well and bring to a boil. Reduce heat, cover and simmer 15-20 minutes.

Once liquid has evaporated, mix with a fork lightly and let sit for a few minutes before serving.

Always remember to remove the bay leaves.

Linda Sue's Hush Puppies

Serves 2 - 4

2 qts vegetable oil for frying
1 (16 oz) can creamed corn
2 eggs, beaten
1 tbsp minced onion
1 1/2 cups self-rising cornmeal
1 tsp seasoning salt

In a deep heavy skillet or deep fryer, heat oil. In a large bowl, combine creamed corn, 2 eggs, minced onion, cornmeal and salt. Mix well and refrigerate for 1-4 hrs.

With a tablespoon, scoop some of the mix and drop into hot oil. Fry 6-8 minutes or until golden brown. Make sure oil is at 375 °F.

Remove from oil and place on a platter lined with paper towels.

Aunt Sue's Hush Puppy Sauce

1/2 cup mayonnaise
1 pinch cayenne pepper
1 tbsp chopped green onions
1 tsp Dijon mustard
1 tsp lemon juice
2 tbsp ketchup
2 tbsp chives
2 tbsp minced red onions
2 tbsp olive oil
2 tbsp sweet relish

Place all ingredients in food processor and blend well, pouring in olive oil slowly.

Southern Fried Okra with Pecans and Remoulade sauce

Serves 4 - 6

1 cup toasted pecans
1 cup cornmeal
1/2 cup flour
3 tbsp Cajun spice blend
1 tsp kosher salt
1/2 tsp pepper
1 lbs frozen whole okra, thawed
2 eggs, well beaten
2 tbsp non-dairy sour cream
oil for frying

In a food processor, mix toasted pecans, cornmeal and flour with Cajun mix. Pulse a few times. Set aside.

Mix egg with sour cream. Dip okra in egg mixture then dip in dry pecan mix. Fry okra 4-6 minutes, remove and place on platter with paper towels.

Remoulade Sauce

3/4 cup mayonnaise
1 1/2 tsp pickle relish
1 tsp finely chopped capers
1 tbsp lemon juice
1 tbsp grainy Dijon mustard
1 tsp regular yellow mustard
2 tsp chopped fresh parsley
2 tbsp ketchup
1/4 tsp fresh tarragon chopped
pinch cayenne pepper
salt to taste

Place all ingredients in the food processor and blend for 1 minute. Serve with the fried okra.

Aunt Sophie's Corned Beef Hash

Serves 4 - 6

2 cups diced corned beef
2 cups russet potatoes, boiled and diced small
1 tsp kosher salt
1 tsp black pepper
1/4 cup canola oil

Heat a large skillet, add oil and diced corned beef. Cook 10-12 minutes. Mash corned beef with a large spoon as it cooks. Once soft, add potatoes and cook until blended well. Try not to purée them.

Keep turning until hot. Add salt and pepper and cover. Let simmer for 5 minutes.

Nir's Tip: To make an unforgettable steak dinner, prepare the corned beef hash and pair it with the London Broil (recipe on page 119). Lay the steak over the corned beef hash, and place 2 poached eggs on top of steak with crispy onions. Wow! You will need to take a nap after dinner!

Southern Succotash

Serves 4 - 6

1/2 lb of frozen baby lima beans
2 tbsp of olive oil
1/4 cup of chopped onions
1/4 cup of chopped green bell pepper
1/2 cup corn fresh or frozen
1 1/2 cups of sliced fresh or frozen okra
1/2 tbsp of granulated sugar
8 oz can whole tomatoes, chopped
1/2 tsp kosher salt
1/4 tsp of freshly cracked black pepper
1 jalapeño seeded and sliced

Cook the lima beans according to the package directions; drain and set aside.

Preheat large heavy skillet. Add olive oil, onions, bell peppers and cook over medium heat until softened.

Add okra to onion and bell pepper; cook for another 5 minutes over medium heat stirring occasionally. Add tomatoes, corn and cook over medium heat for another 5 minutes.

Add lima beans. Reduce heat to medium low and cook 10-15 minutes. Do not overcook the vegetables; you want them al dente.

Season with salt and pepper. For those who like spicy, add jalapeño when adding okra.

You will not be Sufferin' from this Succotash!

SALADS & SOUPS

Duck Confit Salad with Watermelon Croutons

Serves 8-10

8 cups mixed salad greens
1 1/3 cups shredded duck confit
1 avocado cut to cubes
1/2 cup cooked wild rice
1/4 cup sundried cranberries
1/2 cup watermelon croutons
1/2 cup hominy washed and cut if large

Duck Confit

1 whole duck
3 cups stock (veal or chicken)
1 cup orange juice
2 bay leaves

Cut whole duck into quarters and place into a deep oven safe dish. Cover with 3 cups veal or chicken stock. Add 1 cup orange juice and 2 bay leaves. Cover and cook for 2 hours or until the meat begins to fall off the bone. Save the sauce. It will be used to make the dressing.

Pull the meat off the bones, save and refrigerate.

In a saucepan add 1 cup of the stock the duck was cooked in and place in a refrigerator overnight. When cooled, skim as much fat from the top of the stock as possible.

Cranberry Duck Dressing

3/4 cup cranberry preserves
1 cup duck stock
2 tbsp apple cider vinegar
1/4 cup olive oil or less
salt and pepper to taste

In a blender, mix all the ingredients together for a great cranberry duck dressing. Depending on the consistency of the cranberries, vary the amount of duck stock to taste.

Watermelon Croutons

1/2 cup cubed watermelons (1/2 inch cubes)
1 tsp garlic
1 tbsp olive oil
1 tbsp balsamic vinegar

In a heated skillet, add 1 tbsp of olive oil, garlic, balsamic vinegar and bring to a boil. Add watermelon and flip mixture until vinegar has either been absorbed by watermelon or has evaporated. This will happen very quickly. Make sure the watermelon does not lose its shape. Remove and cool.

In a large bowl, add mixed greens, cubed avocado, wild rice, watermelon croutons and hominy. Toss with the cranberry dressing.

Nir's Tip: When pulling apart the duck, I always like to keep the skin on the side. I dry it for a day or 2 in a refrigerator. Then dredge it in cornstarch and deep fry it. You get the best crunchy fried skin. Also, the fat from the duck stock is great for sautéing and frying. Very rich flavor.

Sweet Potato Salad

Serves 8-10

1 cup peeled and cubed sweet potatoes
2 tsp olive oil
1 tsp kosher salt
5 oz baby arugula
5 oz baby spinach
1/4 cup toasted pumpkin seeds
1/4 cup sliced red onions
1/4 cup dry cherries
1/2 cup of lemon poppy dressing

Toss the cubed sweet potatoes in the olive oil and kosher salt. Bake in a preheated oven at 425°F for 20 minutes. Check sweet potatoes for tenderness make sure they don't get too soft. Once cooked, let cool.

Lemon Poppy Dressing

4 oz lemon juice
zest of 1 lemon
3 oz olive oil
1 tsp fresh ground garlic
2 oz tsp white balsamic vinegar
1 tsp sugar
fresh ground black pepper for taste
1 tsp of poppy seeds

In a blender, add all ingredients but the oil. Blend, slowly adding the oil as it mixes.

Mix the arugula, spinach, toasted pumpkin seeds, red onions, dry cherries and sweet potato cubes. Add the lemon poppy dressing and toss.

Purple Potato Salad

Serves 8-10

2 lbs small purple potatoes
1/4 cup chopped green onions
1/2 tsp ground black pepper
1/2 tsp kosher salt
1/2 tsp mustard seeds
1 1/2 tbsp Dijon mustard
1 cup rich mayonnaise
1 large red bell pepper diced
1 large red onion, diced
1/3 cup diced dill pickles
2 hard-cooked eggs, grated
3 celery stalks, sliced small

In a large pot add potatoes and cover with water. Bring to a boil and reduce heat. Cover and simmer for 15-20 minutes. Check for tenderness with a fork. Do not overcook.

Drain thoroughly and cool potatoes. Once cooled, cut potatoes into quarters.

In a large bowl, combine mayonnaise, celery, red bell pepper, onion, pickles, salt, mustard seeds, green onions, Dijon mustard and pepper. Add in potatoes and egg mixing with a ladle in a folding motion. Cover and chill for 6-8 hours. This dish can be made in advance up to a day before.

Nirs Tip: I like to make potato salad the day before I plan to serve it since I may need to add more seasoning, Potatoes absorb flavors, so be prepared.

I love Purple.
This salad makes a fashion food statement!

Grilled Peach and Spinach Salad

Serves 8-10

1/2 cup maple glazed pecans
3 peaches pitted and cut into quarters
2 tsp olive oil
1/4 cup red onions
1/4 cup diced red pepper
7 - 8 oz baby spinach

Spiced Maple Glazed Pecans

2 cups pecans
1/3 cup maple syrup
1/8 tsp kosher salt
1/8 tsp cayenne pepper

Preheat a heavy dry skillet over a medium-high heat. Add the pecans, maple syrup, cayenne pepper and salt. Cook, stirring frequently, until syrup is caramelized and nuts are toasted. Let cool.

Peach Balsamic Dressing

3 quartered peaches
1/2 cup honey
1/3 cup aged balsamic vinegar
1/4 tsp fresh thyme
1/8 tsp black pepper
pinch kosher salt
1/4 cup peach preserves
2 tbsp apple cider vinegar
1/2 cup olive oil

In a small saucepan, bring balsamic vinegar to a boil. Add honey, fresh thyme, black pepper and salt. Let cook until blend is a thick syrup. Remove from heat and let cool. Once cool, place syrup in food processor, add peach preserves, apple cider vinegar and blend. Slowly add olive oil until creamy.

Preheat grill, rub peaches with olive oil and grill for 3-4 minutes on each side. You want the peaches to be tender but not too soft. Let cool.

Toss spinach, red onion, red pepper with peach balsamic dressing and place on large platter. Add grilled peaches on top and sprinkle with spiced pecans.

Beware of your Guest's Nut Allergies;

I'm allergic to some Nuts.

That's why I no longer invite my Neighbor to Dinner!

Coleslaw

Serves 10 - 12

3/4 cup non-dairy sour cream
1/2 cup rich mayonnaise
1/4 cup white wine vinegar
2 tsp sugar
1 tsp celery seed
1 tsp caraway seeds
1 1/2 tsp kosher salt
1/4 tsp cayenne pepper
5 cups shredded green cabbage
4 cups shredded red cabbage
5 medium celery stalks, thinly sliced
2 medium carrots, coarsely grated

Place sour cream, mayonnaise, white vinegar, sugar, salt and cayenne pepper in a food processor. Mix for 30 seconds.

Place caraway seeds, celery seeds and vegetables in large bowl. Add liquid mixture to vegetables. Mix and serve.

Nirs Tip: To add a little more spice, chop up candied pastrami and sprinkle on top.

Macaroni Tuna Salad

Serves 4 - 6

12 -14 oz cooked penne pasta
12 oz canned tuna in water
1/4 cup rich or low fat mayonnaise
1 large chopped kosher dill pickles
3 celery stalks, sliced thin
1 tsp fresh dill
1/2 tsp kosher salt
1/4 tsp black pepper
2 hard-boiled eggs

Cook penne pasta according to package directions. Make sure pasta is al dente and not overcooked. Drain and immediately plunge into cold water to stop any further cooking. Make sure penne is cooled thoroughly.

Drain tuna and coarsely crumble into the pasta. Stir in mayonnaise. Add pickles, celery, fresh dill, salt, pepper, and. grated eggs, saving some grated eggs for garnish on top.

Recipe can be made in advance and stored in a refrigerator for later use.

If you're intimidated by this recipe,

you are   of the Sea !

Kale and Collard Green Salad with Pears and Creamy Garlic Dressing

Serves 8 - 10

1 bunch fresh collard greens
1 bunch Tuscan kale
3/4 cup sweet dried cranberries
3 Bartlett pears, sliced
2 avocados, peeled and diced
1/2 cup shredded red cabbage
3/4 cup chopped toasted pecans
4 tbsp crispy pastrami (recipe on page 80)
1 cup creamy garlic dressing

Creamy Garlic Dressing

1 tbsp Dijon mustard
1 tbsp fresh dill
1 tbsp chopped fresh basil
1 tbsp. onion powder
1 tsp garlic powder
1/2 tsp fresh cracked black pepper
1/2 tsp kosher salt
2 tbsp extra virgin olive oil
2 tbsp crushed garlic
4 tbsp fresh lemon juice
4 tbsp milk substitute
5 oz non-dairy cream cheese

Place all ingredients in a blender and mix until it reaches a creamy consistency.

In a large mixing bowl, toss the collard greens, Tuscan kale, sweet dried cranberries, sliced pears, avocado, red cabbage and toss with dressing. Top with pecans and serve.

Nir's Tip: Collard greens and kale are a tougher green leaf. I always recommend pre-dressing them at least 15- 20 minutes before you eat to soften and give more flavor to the green leaves. Tuscan Kale is also called Lacinato Kale.

Split Pea Soup with Crispy Pastrami Bits

Serves 4 - 6

1/2 tbsp olive oil
2 cups chopped yellow onions
6 oz fatty pastrami sliced thick, chopped into small pieces
1/2 tbsp kosher salt
1 tsp freshly ground black pepper
1 tbsp fresh chopped garlic
2 bay leaves
16 oz dried green split peas, rinsed
8 cups chicken broth
1/2 cup non-dairy creamer
1/2 cup non-dairy cream cheese

Heat a large pot over medium–high heat. Add oil and chopped pastrami and stir so it does not burn. Save some pastrami on the side for garnish. Add onions and sauté 3-4 minutes. Add garlic, bay leaves, and split peas and cook, stirring, for 2 minutes. Add chicken broth and bring to a boil.

Once soup boils, add salt, pepper, non-dairy creamer and non-dairy cream cheese. Reduce heat to medium and simmer, stirring occasionally for 45 minutes until the peas are tender. Remove from heat and let cool slightly. Remove and discard bay leaves.

For a creamy texture, use a hand held immersion blender and blend until soup is smooth. Once soup cools, you may need to add water or more broth when reheating.

Crispy Pastrami

1 lb pastrami sliced medium thick
non-stick oil spray

Dice the pastrami very small. Heat up a heavy duty skillet with a medium to high temperature, and spray oil. Do not use a Teflon pan, as you will not get the same crispy texture. Once you add pastrami keep mixing every 60 seconds so it does not stick to the pan. Continue cooking until pastrami gets nice and dark but not burned.

Remove and drain. Use for salads, soups or anything you like.

Nir's Tip: A great substitute for the pastrami is the turkey pastrami. But remember, the turkey is drier, so you may need to cut it thicker and mix it faster, so it does not stick.

Chicken Soup with Collard Green Matzo Balls

Serves 10-12

1 large roasting chicken (3 1/2 - 4 lbs)
5 qts of water
4 stalks of celery cut into 1" pieces
3 large carrots peeled and cut into slices
1 large onion, peeled and cut
1 green zucchini cut into 1/4" slices
1 large parsnip cut into slices
2 whole tomato
2 tbsp chopped dill
3 bay leaves
fresh ground pepper
kosher salt to taste
1/4 cup julienne cut carrots and zucchini

In a large pot add 5 qts of water, chicken, celery, carrots, onions, zucchini, parsnips, bay leaves, pepper, tomato and bring to a boil. Remove foam that collects on top. Reduce heat and let cook 1 1/2-2 hours uncovered. During last hour add fresh dill. Flavor as needed.

Remove chicken and let cool. Strain the soup and remove vegetables and discard. Set soup aside to cool then refrigerate overnight. Remove congealed fat the next day.

When reheating soup, put in cup of raw julienne vegetables and serve.

Collard Green Matzo Balls

Makes 12

1 1/2 cups matzo meal
6 large eggs beaten
3 tbsp canola oil
2 tbsp chopped collard greens
1 tsp kosher salt

Mix all ingredients in a medium bowl. Cover and refrigerate for 2 hours or overnight.

Add 4 qts of water with salt to a medium size pot and bring to a boil. Take chilled mixture from refrigerator and with an oiled hand form 12 even sized balls. Drop matzo balls into boiling water and reduce to medium heat. Cover pot and let cook for 15-20 minutes. Make sure matzo balls are still firm.

Remove and place directly in bowls of hot chicken soup and serve.

Chicken Soup with Beef Dumplings

Serves 10-12

1 large roasting chicken (3 1/2 - 4 lbs)
5 qts of water
4 stalks of celery cut into 1" pieces
3 large carrots peeled and cut into slices
1 large onion, peeled and cut
1 green zucchini cut into 1/4" slices
1 large parsnip cut into slices
2 whole tomatoes
2 tbsp chopped dill
3 bay leaves
fresh ground pepper
kosher salt to taste
1/4 cup julienne cut carrots and zucchini

In a large pot add 5 qts. water, chicken, celery, carrots, onions, zucchini, parsnips, bay leaves, pepper and tomatoes and bring to a boil. Remove foam that collects on top. Reduce heat and let cook 1 1/2-2 hours uncovered. During last hour add fresh dill. Flavor as needed.

Remove chicken and let cool. Strain the soup and remove vegetables and discard. Set soup aside to cool then refrigerate overnight. Remove congealed fat the next day. When re-heating soup, put in cup of raw julienne vegetables and serve.

Beef Dumplings

1 3/4 cups flour
2 eggs
1/2 tsp kosher salt
3 tbsp oil
1 cup ground cooked beef or chicken
1 small onion, grated
1 clove garlic
1 tsp parsley
1 tsp kosher salt

In a large bowl combine dough ingredients. Knead and roll out on floured board and cut into 3" squares or circles.

Mix filling ingredients well. With a tsp, take 1/2 spoonful of filling and place in center of the cut dough. Press ends firmly with fingers or fork. Dumpling can now be either boiled in separate pot or boiled in the soup itself and served.

Place in boiling salted water. Cook approximately 15-20 minutes until dumplings float to top.

Nir's Tip: Dumplings can be made a few days ahead of time and saved frozen, either raw or cooked. Remove frozen and boil or if cooked, put in soup while warming up.

Southern Corn and Potato Chowder

Serves 4 - 6

5 cups cooked corn
4 cups diced potatoes
2 tbsp unsalted margarine
1 cup onion, diced
2 tbsp non-dairy cream cheese
1/2 tbsp fresh dill
2 1/2 tsp kosher salt
1 tsp onion powder
1/2 tsp white pepper
4 cups water
4 cups milk substitute
3 tbsp of roux

In a stockpot add margarine and onions. Sauté onions until golden brown. Add corn which has been thoroughly drained. Add potatoes and sauté for another 5 minutes. Add 4 cups of water and bring to a boil. Make sure water covers potatoes.

Once potatoes are tender, add milk substitute, non-dairy cream cheese, roux, dill, onion powder, salt and white pepper and bring to a boil, stirring continuously.

Once soup comes to a boil reduce heat and let simmer for another 25-30 minutes. Top with shredded non-dairy cheese and serve.

The pan is fine.
My husband? Eh, not so much.

POULTRY

Smothered Fried Chicken with Waffles and Grits

Serves 6 - 8

Fried Chicken

2 large whole chickens cut into eighths
1 cup all purpose flour
1 cup cornstarch
1 tbsp garlic powder
1 tbsp onion powder
1 tsp kosher salt
1 tsp ground pepper
1 tsp paprika
3 eggs

In a bowl combine mayonnaise and egg. Dip chicken in mixture and coat completely, set aside.

In another bowl, add flour, cornstarch, garlic powder, onion powder, paprika, salt and pepper. Place chicken pieces in mixture one at a time to coat. Add more flour and cornstarch as necessary.

In a deep-fryer or large saucepan, heat the oil to 375 °F. Be sure to use enough oil to cover chicken pieces. Place coated chicken on a platter. The mixture of the egg, mayonnaise, flour, and cornstarch will create a doughy consistency. After a few minutes, the chicken is ready to be fried. Once chicken is doughy, place in the oil, two or three pieces at a time. The more chicken you add to the oil, the more the temperature will decrease, causing the chicken to cook longer and absorb more oil.

Fry chicken 8-12 minutes or until cooked through. Check with a food thermometer in the thickest part and make sure the temperature reads 170 -175 °F.

Nir's Tip: Frying too many pieces at a time decreases oil temperature. This causes chicken to cook longer, and absorb more oil.

Gravy

1 tsp of tomato paste
1 tsp soy sauce
1/2 tsp chopped fresh sage
1 tsp minced garlic
1/2 tsp rough chopped fresh thyme
2 tbsp canola oil or olive oil
2 tbsp minced shallots
3 cups beef broth
6 tbsp roux
1 tsp kosher salt
1 tsp freshly ground black pepper

Heat oil in a saucepan over medium heat. Add roux and sauté 4-5 minutes. Roux will soften and get darker with a nice toasty smell.

Add shallots, garlic, thyme, sage and soy sauce and continue to cook, stirring for 3 minutes. Add beef broth, tomato paste and season with salt and pepper. Bring to a boil and mix vigorously with a whisk until liquid thickens. Lower heat and simmer until sauce has reduced (15-20 minutes).

Waffles

Makes 6 - 8

2 cups flour
1 tbsp baking powder
2 tsp white sugar
3/4 tbsp kosher salt
2 large eggs, beaten
1 1/2 cups warm almond milk or soymilk
5 tbsp margarine, melted
1 tbsp tofutti sour cream

Preheat a waffle iron. In a medium-sized bowl, sift together flour, baking powder, sugar, and salt. In another bowl, whisk together eggs, almond milk, margarine and sour cream until well mixed. Whisk liquids into dry ingredients until blended well.

Ladle the batter into preheated waffle iron, pushing the batter to the edges of the iron. Cook until golden brown.

Place the waffle on the plate, take a large spoon and put the warm grits on the waffle. Pour the gravy over the grits and then place fried chicken on top. If you pour gravy on the chicken, you lose the crispiness.

Grits

1 1/2 cups water
3/4 cup almond milk or soy milk
1/4 cup non-dairy cream cheese
3 tbsp unsalted margarine
1/2 tsp kosher salt
1/4 tsp freshly ground white pepper
3/4 cup yellow or white corn grits

In a medium pot, add water and salt. Stir in grits and bring to a boil. Turn down heat and let cook 30-40 minutes, stirring often. Add almond milk, non-dairy cream cheese, margarine and white pepper and let simmer. Whisk the grits until smooth, adding almond/soy milk as needed to reach the desired consistency.

Forget the Diet
Just try it
you know you want to . . .

Chicken Pot Pie

Serves 8 - 10

1 whole chicken (3 1/2 - 4 lbs)
6 tbsp olive oil
3 tsp kosher salt
1 tsp freshly ground black pepper
7 cups chicken stock
2 cups yellow onions, chopped
1/2 cup of roux
1/4 cup non-dairy cream cheese
1/4 cup non-dairy sour cream
2 cups medium-diced carrots, blanched and cooled
1 cup diced celery
2 cups frozen peas
1 1/2 cups small whole pearl onions
1/2 cup minced fresh parsley leaves
6 pieces of puff pastry dough, 7-8 inches circle
1 egg with 2 tsp water whipped for egg wash

Preheat the oven to 350°F.

Cut whole chicken into eighths. Place on a baking sheet and rub with 3 tbsp of olive oil, salt and pepper and roast for 35 to 40 minutes or until cooked through. Set the chicken aside until cool. Remove meat from bones. Discard skin and bones. Cut up chicken into small cubes. This should yield about 4 cups.

In a small pot, heat the chicken stock separately. In a larger pot that will hold all ingredients, heat 3 tbsp of olive oil and sauté chopped onions, celery and diced carrots over medium-low heat for 10-15 minutes until onions are a light golden brown. Add hot chicken stock and roux. Bring to a boil while mixing with a whisk. Once roux has dissolved, simmer over low heat for 2 more minutes, stirring, until thick. Add 2 tsp salt, 1 tsp pepper, cream cheese, sour cream, chicken, peas, whole pearl onions and parsley. Mix well. Let cook another 15 minutes.

Raise the oven temperature to 375°F.

Divide the filling equally among 6 ovenproof bowls. Sprinkle flour on rolling pin and roll out the 7 inch round pastry dough a few times to flatten dough. Pierce the dough with a fork. This will protect the pastry dough from rising while baking.

Brush the outside edges of each bowl with the egg wash and place the dough on top of bowl. The pastry circle should reach 1/2 inch over the edge of bowl on all sides. Crimp dough and press to make it stick. Brush the dough with egg wash. Make a small hole in the center of the dough. This will let the steam out. The hole should not be larger than a pea.

Place the pies on a baking sheet and bake for 45 minutes to 1 hour, or until the top is golden brown and the pie filling is bubbling.

Tarragon Lemon Chicken

Serves 4

1 whole chicken (3 1/2 - 4 lbs)
2 tbsp fresh tarragon, chopped
2 tbsp fresh lemon juice
3 whole lemons halved
zest of 1 lemon
2 tbsp chopped garlic
1/3 cup olive oil
1 tsp kosher salt
1 tsp black pepper

Preheat oven to 375°F.

In a large bowl, mix tarragon, lemon juice, lemon zest, garlic, olive oil, salt and pepper. Rub chicken all over with marinade. It is important to separate the skin from the flesh, rubbing marinade under the skin. Do not remove skin. Let chicken sit covered in a refrigerator for a few hours or overnight.

Remove from refrigerator 30 minutes before roasting and place in roasting pan. Place one of the halved lemons in the cavity of chicken, the rest under the chicken. With butcher twine, tie the legs together. Place in oven. After 35-40 minutes, baste the chicken with its own juices from the roasting pan. Roast for another 10-15 minutes. Check with a thermometer in the thick part of the thigh. The correct temperature should be between 170 - 175 °F.

Let rest for a few minutes before cutting..

Nir's Tip: Add some small new potatoes and baby vegetables to the roasting pan of the chicken, and by the time the chicken is ready, you have your sides.

Pounded Chicken Breast with Cajun Mayo Dipping Sauce

Serves 4

1 tsp minced fresh thyme leaves
1 tsp finely grated lemon zest
1 tsp fresh minced rosemary
3/4 tsp kosher salt
1 tsp freshly ground black pepper
1 cup all-purpose flour for dredging
2 large eggs, beaten
4 boneless skinless chicken breasts, each about 6 ounces
3/4 cup oil for frying
1 cup panko bread crumbs

In a food processor blend panko, thyme, rosemary, lemon zest, salt and pepper. With smooth side of a meat-mallet, pound each breast to equal thickness. Put flour, eggs and panko bread crumbs in 3 separate dishes. Pat the chicken dry and season with salt and pepper. Dip each breast into flour and shake off the excess. Dip cutlet in beaten egg to coat it lightly. Lay chicken in panko, turn and press with the palm of your hand into breading to coat both sides.

Heat a large skillet over medium heat. Fill skillet half way up with oil. Lay chicken breasts in pan. Cook chicken without turning for about 4 minutes until brown. Turn chicken and cook until equally brown on other side. Transfer chicken to a plate with paper towel.

Cajun Mayo Dipping Sauce

1/2 cup mayonnaise
2 tbsp non-dairy creamer or soy/almond milk
2 tbsp Cajun spice mix
1 tbsp hot sauce
1 tsp of lemon juice
salt to taste

Mix all ingredients in a bowl with a whisk and place in serving bowl.

Georgia Peach Chicken

Serves 6

6 boneless, skinless chicken breasts - about 2 1/2 lbs
1/2 cup brown sugar
1/2 cup Chef Nir's non-dairy ranch dressing
1 can (16 oz) sliced peaches, drained and cut into small chunks
1 tbsp olive oil
1 tsp pepper
1 tsp kosher salt
2 tbsp Dijon mustard
3 tbsp olive oil

Preheat large heavy skillet over a medium flame. Add olive oil. Sprinkle chicken breasts with salt and pepper and sauté for 5-6 minutes per side.

Remove chicken from skillet. In the same skillet, add 1 tbsp of olive oil and brown sugar. Stir in Nir's non-dairy ranch dressing and mustard, stirring while heating.

Return chicken to pan with the cut peaches; cook 10-12 minutes with sauce and heat through.

Chef Nir's Non-Dairy Ranch Dressing

1/2 cup non-dairy sour cream
1 tsp apple cider vinegar
1 cup mayonnaise
2 tsp chopped fresh garlic
1 tsp garlic powder
3 tbsp chopped green onions
1 tbsp onion powder
1 tsp dry thyme
1 tsp freshly ground pepper

Place all ingredients in a food processor and blend for 2 minutes. Add 1-2 tbsp of any true non-dairy creamer, almond milk or soy milk if still too thick.

Nir's Tip: This recipe is great for the person who is lactose intolerant. Great for salads, sandwiches and dips. One thing about Kosher is there is no percentage for mistake. If it says non-dairy, it will be 100% dairy-free. Not like some non-dairy products that say non-dairy, but have sometimes 1% dairy in them or are made in dairy equipment.

In our restaurant, we have many clients who are not Kosher, but they say, only in Kosher restaurants, can they be assured that everything they eat is all 100% non-dairy.

Best when served with
Mint Julep iced tea
See y'all out on the porch!

Pulled Chicken BBQ Sandwich

Serves 4

3 tbsp canola oil
1 whole chicken, 3 - 3 1/2 lbs
1 large onion, sliced
1 cup BBQ sauce
1/2 cup water
1 tsp brown sugar
1 tsp ground garlic
salt & pepper to taste
demi-baguette - 8 inches

Cut whole chicken into eighths. Place chicken on a baking sheet and rub with 3 tbsp of canola oil, salt and pepper. Roast for 35-40 minutes or until cooked through.

Set the chicken aside until cool enough to handle, then remove the meat from the bones and discard the skin and bones. Either shred or cut chicken into small cubes. This should yield about 4 cups of chicken.

Preheat heavy skillet and sauté onions until soft. Add chicken and sauté for a few more minutes. Once hot, add barbecue sauce, garlic, water, sugar, and stir very well. Cover and cook on medium heat 15-20 minutes.

Cut Bun/Baguette and add pulled chicken.

Deep Fried Matzo Meal Chicken Cutlets

Serves 8

8 boneless, skinless chicken breasts
3 eggs beaten
1 cup potato starch
2 cups matzo meal
1 tsp onion powder
1 tsp garlic powder
1 tsp kosher salt
1/2 tsp black pepper
1/2 tsp dry thyme

Make sure chicken cutlets are not too thick. Fill large skillet to 1/3 with oil and preheat to 375 °F.

Season the matzo meal with onion powder, garlic powder, kosher salt, black pepper and thyme. Dredge the cutlets in the potato starch, shake off the extra starch, dip in the egg, and then dip in the seasoned matzo meal. Place in oil and fry for 8-10 minutes, turning cutlets half way through. When done, drain on tray with paper towel.

Nir's Tip: This dish is great for Passover. If using this recipe for Passover, make sure all the ingredients are Kosher for Passover.

PASSOVER APPROVED

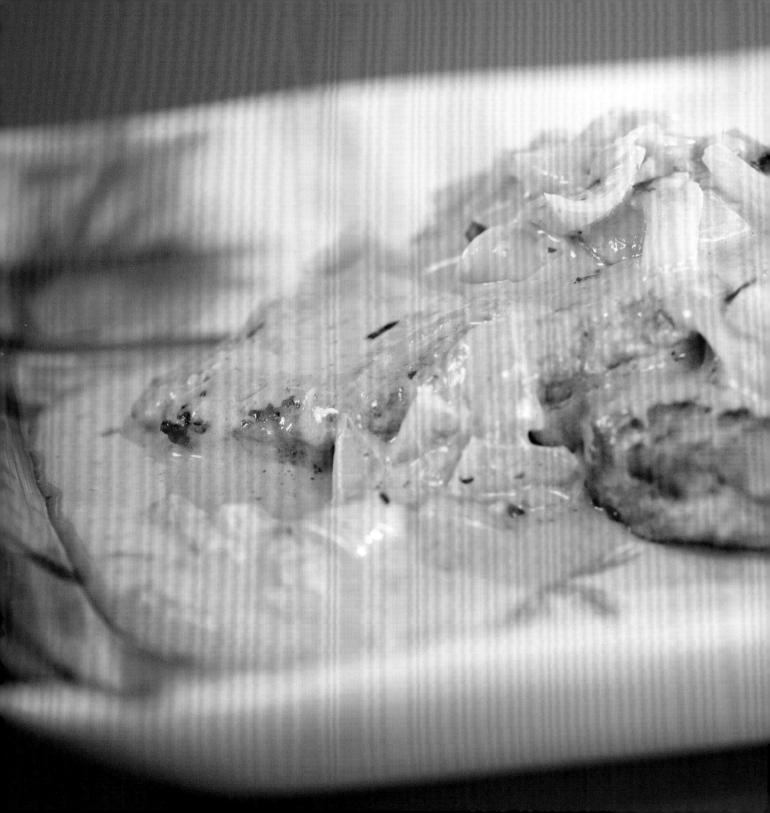

Smothered Turkey Cutlets

Serves 4

4 turkey breast cutlets
1 1/4 cup chicken stock
1 tbsp roux
1 tbsp non-dairy sour cream
2 tbsp minced parsley
2 tbsp olive oil
6 oz diced onions
1 tsp kosher salt
1 tsp pepper

Place 1 turkey cutlet between 2 sheets of wax paper and lightly flatten with a mallet. Spread flour on a plate and season with salt and pepper. Dredge the cutlets with the flour, patting the flour into both sides.

Add oil to a heavy skillet and heat over medium heat. Add cutlets and sauté 2 cutlets at a time, 3 minutes on each side until golden and cooked through.

Transfer the cutlets to a platter and reduce the temperature of the skillet. Add onions and sauté 3-4 minutes. Add 1 cup stock and roux and bring to a boil, whisking constantly. When the sauce is thickened, reduce the heat and stir in the sour cream and parsley until blended. Season with salt and pepper. Use the extra stock to dilute the gravy.

Return the turkey cutlets to the gravy. Let cook for another 5-8 minutes on a low heat.

Fresh Roasted Turkey

Serves 8 - 10

1/2 cup canola oil
2 tsp chopped sage very coarse
1 fresh turkey (10 -12 lbs)
2 tbsp kosher salt
2 tbsp freshly ground black pepper
1 large bunch fresh thyme
1 whole lemon, cut in half
1 tbsp chopped fresh rosemary
2 tbsp chopped garlic

Preheat the oven to 350°F.

Add chopped sage, black pepper, rosemary and garlic to canola oil and set aside. Wash turkey inside and out. Remove any excess fat and pat the outside dry. Place the turkey in a large roasting pan breast down. Liberally salt and pepper the inside of turkey cavity.

Stuff the cavity with the bunch of fresh thyme, halved lemon and garlic. Brush the outside of the turkey with herb and oil mixture and sprinkle with salt and pepper. Using your hands, massage under the skin with the herb mixture making sure herbs remain under the skin. Tie the legs together with string.

Roast the turkey 20 minutes per pound, about 3-3 1/2 hours, or until the juices run clear when you cut between the leg and the thigh. Remove the turkey to a cutting board and cover with aluminum foil. Let rest for 20 minutes.

Cranberry Ginger Relish

1 (16-oz) bag fresh cranberries
1 2/3 cups sugar
1/2 tsp fresh ground ginger
1 cup orange juice
1 cup water
1/2 tsp lemon zest

Combine cranberries, sugar, ginger, orange juice and water in a medium saucepan over medium heat. Bring to a boil and simmer until most cranberries are broken up, about 20 minutes.

Stir in lemon zest and continue simmering until thick. Remove from heat, cool and refrigerate. Best prepared the day before serving.

Herb Bread Stuffing

1/4 cup finely chopped onions
1/2 cup sliced mushrooms
1/2 cup chopped celery
1/4 cup canola oil plus 2 tbsp for sauté
4 cups toasted sourdough bread cubes
1/8 tsp pepper
2 eggs, beaten
1/2 tsp kosher salt
1/4 to 1/2 tsp ground sage
1 tsp black pepper
chicken broth or vegetable broth

Heat a large skillet over medium heat and add 2 tbsp oil.

Sauté onions, celery and mushrooms until softened. Combine mixture with bread cubes, eggs, salt, black pepper and sage in a large bowl. Stir in broth until well moistened. In a greased covered roasting pan or a casserole dish add mixture and bake in a preheated oven at 350 °F for 35-45 minutes. Take the cover off for the last 5 minutes to brown the top of stuffing.

Nir's Tip: For a great stuffing, make sure the sourdough bread is toasted. If not toasted the stuffing becomes mushy.

Beef, Lamb & Veal

London Broil

Serves 4-6

2 1/2 lbs London Broil
1/2 cup dry red wine
2 tbsp olive oil
2 tbsp soy sauce
1 tbsp whole oregano
1 tbsp brown sugar
1 tsp coarsely ground black pepper
1 tbsp ground garlic
1/2 tsp kosher salt

Place meat in a large plastic freezer bag.

Combine red wine, olive oil, soy sauce, mustard, brown sugar, salt, pepper, and garlic. Pour the marinade into bag with steak, seal and place inside a large dish to prevent spills. Marinate and refrigerate for 6-24 hours.

Preheat a gas or charcoal grill to high heat. Remove steak from the marinade and place on grill. Cook 6 minutes per side for rare. Transfer the steak to a cutting board and let stand for 5 minutes before carving.

I'll never know why they call this London Broil it should be called Jersey Broil because We Love It!

Prime Rib Roast with Au Jus

Serves 8 - 10

7 - 8 lbs prime rib roast
3 tbsp sea salt
1 1/2 tbsp coarsely cracked black pepper
2 tbsp extra-virgin olive oil
8 sprigs fresh rosemary
8 sprigs fresh thyme
2 tbsp fresh ground garlic
1/4 cup vegetable oil
1 tbsp fresh cracked pepper
1 cup red wine
1 cup beef broth

Preheat oven to 375°F.

Tie rib roast with butchers twine. Add rosemary, thyme, and rub with garlic, salt and pepper.

Heat a large skillet for 2 minutes. Add olive oil and sear beef on all outer sides (not the cut sides). Transfer the beef to roasting pan.

Roast the beef until a thermometer inserted into the center reads 120–125°F for rare. For medium-rare, 130-135°F and for medium, 140–145°F. Cover and set aside.

Remove the roast from the roasting pan and place pan on the stove over medium heat. Add beef stock and deglaze the bottom of roasting pan to get the drippings. Heat a small pan on high, add wine and let the alcohol evaporate. Boil for 2-3 minutes and add beef stock with the drippings. Reduce heat and bring to a reduction. Let the meat rest while you make the au jus.

Creamy Horseradish Sauce

4 tbsp prepared horseradish
1 tbsp white vinegar
1/2 tsp dry mustard powder
1/2 cup mayonnaise
1/2 cup non dairy sour cream
1/2 tsp onion powder

In a food processor, add all ingredients and blend for 2-3 minutes.

Nir's Tip: Take the beef out of the refrigerator 2 hours before cooking so it can warm to room temperature. After 30 minutes, season the meat on all sides with the sea salt and cracked black pepper.

Oxtails

Serves 6 - 8

3 lb oxtails
1 onion cut in quarters
8 garlic cloves
4 cups chicken broth
1 tbsp seasoning salt
1 tbsp black pepper
4 tbsp white vinegar
2 tbsp all purpose flour
1 can (16 oz) of crushed tomatoes

Start by cleaning the extra fat off the oxtails.

Season the meat on all sides with salt and pepper and dredge in flour. Sear oxtails on all sides; remove from the pan and set aside. Add garlic and onions and cook over medium-high heat for 5 minutes. Add vinegar.

Deglaze the pan by adding 1 cup of broth. Use a wooden spoon to scrape any bits from the bottom of the pan. Add the crushed tomatoes and cook for 15 minutes. Place oxtails in pot. Add remainder of stock to cover the oxtails.

Cover pan and bring to a boil. Simmer for 2-3 hours or until meat falls off the bone.

Beef Brisket

Serves 6 - 8

5 lbs beef brisket
1 tsp kosher salt
1 tbsp fresh ground black pepper
1 tbsp sweet paprika
2 tsp dried oregano
3 tbsp vegetable oil
3 1/2 cups low veal or beef stock
1 can (16 oz) chopped tomatoes
2 bay leaves
3 medium yellow onions, sliced thin
1 tbsp chopped garlic

Preheat oven to 350°F.

Combine salt, pepper, paprika and oregano in small bowl. Rub spice mixture over meat.

Heat oil in oven proof pot with a tight-fitting lid, over medium-high heat. Sear brisket on both sides.

Add stock, tomatoes and bay leaves to pot and scrape the brown bits off the bottom of the pot.

Scatter onions and garlic and cover pot, transfer to oven and braise for 2 1/2 to 3 hours.

Brisket is done when the meat is extremely tender.

When serving, add onions, tomatoes and juices on top of brisket.

Honey Glazed Mustard Seed Brisket

Serves 6 - 8

4 lbs center-cut beef brisket, trimmed
2 tbsp canola oil
2 tsp kosher salt
2 tsp black pepper
4 medium onions, thinly sliced
2 cloves garlic, thinly sliced
1/2 cup honey
1/4 cup Dijon mustard
1/4 cup dry white wine
1/2 tsp dried thyme leaves, crushed
2 tsp mustard seeds

Sprinkle both sides of brisket with salt, pepper and mustard seeds. Heat large skillet and add oil. Sear brisket on all sides. Remove to platter. Add onions and garlic to pan and cook until golden and slightly softened.

Preheat oven to 350°F.

In small bowl, whisk together honey, mustard, wine and thyme. Return brisket to pan and place on top of onions. Pour juices from brisket platter and 3/4 of honey-wine mixture over brisket. Add 1 cup of water to pan and bring to a boil. Cover and transfer to oven. Bake for 2 1/2 – 3 hours, basting with pan juices every 20 to 30 minutes.

Uncover and pour remaining honey-wine mixture over brisket. Onion mixture will be a dark bronze color at this point. Bake uncovered for another 20 minutes.

Remove brisket to platter and let sit 15 minutes. To serve, slice brisket across grain. Serve with onions and drizzle with pan juices.

Rack of Lamb

Serves 2 - 4

2 lbs Rack of Lamb

Jalapeño Mint Sauce with Cardamom and Minced Garlic

1/2 cup washed mint
1 large seeded jalapeño
1 tbsp chopped garlic
1/2 tsp fresh ground cardamom
2 tbsp honey
1 tbsp light corn syrup
1 tsp kosher salt
1/4 cup olive oil

Place all sauce ingredients in food processor and purée until mixture is smooth.

Preheat oven to 375°F.

Once rack of lamb has been cleaned, rub with Jalapeño Mint Sauce on both sides. Marinate and refrigerate for 2-4 hours.

Remove lamb from refrigerator and allow to reach room temperature. Preheat a heavy skillet and add oil. Sear lamb on both sides for 3-4 minutes. Place in oven for 6-10 minutes until meat reaches desired temperature. Check with meat thermometer. Let sit for 5 minutes, carve and serve.

Breaded Veal Chop

Serves 4

4 veal chops, bone-in
1/2 cup flour
2 eggs
1 cup seasoned bread crumbs
1/2 tsp fresh rosemary coarsely chopped
1/2 tsp fresh thyme
3/4 cup oil for frying

Pat the veal chops dry.

In a shallow bowl, whisk the eggs. In another bowl, place the seasoned bread crumbs.

Add a little chopped rosemary and thyme to the seasoned bread crumbs and mix well.

Dip chops in flour and then in egg batter, letting any excess egg drip off. Pat the bread crumbs into the chop.

Heat a heavy skillet over medium heat and add oil.

Fry chops until golden brown on one side for 8 minutes then turn and continue to fry for another 7-8 minutes.

Nir's note: Squeeze fresh lemon juice over veal chop and sprinkle with sea salt.

Short Ribs in Spicy Pineapple Sauce

Serves 4 - 6

2 1/2 lbs full-size, bone-in beef short ribs
fresh pineapple, cored, and cut into 1 inch pieces
1/2 cup soy sauce
1/4 cup apple cider vinegar
1 tbsp honey
1 tsp sized piece of ginger, peeled
1 tbsp lime juice
1 tbsp fresh garlic
1 tsp onion powder
1 tbsp Chinese 5 spice powder

Preheat a large skillet.

Sear all sides of the short ribs and place in a dish deep enough for the ribs and the sauce for braising in the oven.

Blend all above ingredients until smooth, and pour over the meat in the braising dish.

Cook at 275-300 °F for 5- 6 hours.

The long and short
of it, these Ribs
can't be Beat!

Beef Stew

Serves 8 - 10

4 tbsp olive oil
2 tsp chopped garlic
2 lbs trimmed beef chuck, cut into 1-2 inch cubes,
patted dry with paper towels
1/4 cup of flour
10-15 small red potatoes
1 medium onion, chopped
2 cups sliced carrots
1 cup corn (fresh or frozen)
2 cups sliced celery
1 cup of red cooking wine
2 1/2 cups beef stock or veal stock
1 can (16 oz) diced tomatoes, drained
4 bay leaves
1/2 tsp fresh thyme
1 tbsp chopped parsley
1/2 tsp allspice
1 tsp paprika
1 cup sliced shitake mushrooms
2 tbsp roux

Preheat a deep skillet. Add olive oil and heat on medium-high.
Add beef which has been dredged in flour and sauté until
the beef gets a nice golden coating. Add red wine, mix well
and continue to boil for 10-15 minutes. Add potatoes, onions,
carrots, corn and celery.

Let cook for another 5-10 minutes and add thyme,
parsley, allspice and paprika. Sauté and add mushrooms. After
mushrooms soften, add broth and diced tomato with juice. Mix
well and add the bay leaves. Bring to a boil. Keep covered and
simmer for 2-4 hours. Meat should be very tender and tasty.

Nir's Tip: Wine can be substituted with grape juice, apple juice or
by simply increasing the beef broth to 2 cups. I prefer to use red
cooking wine as it adds a wonderful flavor!

Meatloaf

Serves 4 - 6

2 1/2 lbs ground beef
1/2 tsp garlic powder
1/2 tsp onion powder
1 pinch of kosher salt
1 pinch of pepper
1 cup seasoned bread crumbs
1 medium egg
3 medium eggs - hard boiled

Place ground meat in a large bowl. Add garlic powder, onion powder and bread crumbs. Season with salt and pepper and add egg. Mix thoroughly. Use hands to shape meat.

Lightly grease a flat baking dish. Put the meat in the middle and form into a log. Make an elongated cavity in the middle, stuff with hard-boiled eggs. Cover eggs completely.

Bake for 1 - 1 1/2 hours until the meat is completely cooked.

We aren't talking about the
Rock Star "here"... this
American Dish
has its own tune!

Pasta Carbonara

Serves 3 - 4

1 lb dry spaghetti
2 tbsp extra-virgin olive oil
4 oz pastrami, cubed or sliced into small strips
1 tsp roux
1 tbsp chopped garlic
1 large egg plus 1 egg yolk
1/2 cup non-dairy cream cheese
1 tbsp chopped Italian parsley
freshly ground black pepper and salt to taste

Bring a large pot of salted water to a boil, add pasta and cook for 8-10 minutes or until al dente. Drain pasta well, reserving 1/2 cup of the starchy cooking water.

Beat eggs and non-dairy cream cheese in a mixing bowl. Set aside.

Heat olive oil in a deep skillet over medium heat and add pastrami. Sauté until pastrami is crisp. Add garlic and roux and sauté briefly to soften.

Add drained spaghetti to pan and mix well for 2 minutes.

Reduce heat and pour egg/cheese mixture into pasta, mixing quickly until the eggs thicken, but do not scramble. Reduce to low heat to ensure this does not happen. Thin the sauce with a bit of the reserved pasta water as needed. Season the carbonara with freshly ground black pepper and salt to taste. Serve in a large bowl, garnished with chopped parsley.

Nir's Tip: Prepare the sauce while the pasta is cooking to ensure that the spaghetti will be hot and ready when the sauce is finished. It is very important that the pasta is hot when adding the egg mixture, so that the heat of the pasta cooks the raw eggs in the sauce.

Homemade Semolina Pasta

Makes 1 1/2 lbs of pasta

2 1/2 cups semolina flour
4 large eggs, whisked
water

Place semolina flour in bowl of an electric mixer, using the dough hook. Begin mixing. Slowly pour eggs while mixing until dough comes together. If dough seems a little dry, add a few tsp of water until dough feels smooth.

Transfer dough to flat surface and using your hands, knead the dough for a few minutes. Form a round shape with the dough and cover with plastic wrap. Let sit for 30 minutes.

Pasta can be rolled out with a rolling pin or cut into small balls and run through a pasta machine.

Once you roll out pasta, it can be cut into any size or shape. Let dry for at least 30 minutes.

Storing fresh pasta: Wrapped loosely in a plastic bag, fresh pasta will keep for 3 days refrigerated. Wrap tightly in a second bag and freeze for up to a month.

Nir's Tip: When you cook fresh pasta, allow 4-6 quarts of water per pound. Fresh pasta cooks quickly, so cook no longer than 3-4 minutes. Bring water and 1 tbsp salt to a boil. Do not cook more than 2 lbs at a time. Separate pasta and add to boiling water, stir and begin timing. Once pasta is cooked, drain well and toss immediately with the sauce, coating evenly.

To cook frozen pasta: Do not thaw. Place directly from freezer into boiling water and stir until separated. Allow extra time to become tender.

My Kosher PLT

Serves 4

1 lb crispy pastrami
8 lettuce leaves
2 large tomatoes sliced
4 tsp of my spicy peach ketchup
2 tsp mayonnaise
8 slices of bread

Toast the bread. Spread the spicy peach ketchup on one side and the mayonnaise on the other side. Take one slice and stack lettuce and tomatoes and top with the crispy pastrami. Cover with remaining slice.

Spicy Peach Ketchup

8 tbsp of ketchup
4 tbsp peach preserves
1 tsp Tabasco or any spicy sauce

Great for dipping anything. Replace the peachy ketchup with Jalapeño Mint Sauce (recipe on page 125) to add an extra bite.

Steak Burger with Pulled Beef and Spicy Mayo

Serves 4 - 6

2 lbs ground chuck steak (20-30% fat)
2 lbs pulled beef (recipe on page 38)
1 lb crispy pastrami (recipe on page 76)
1/2 tsp freshly ground black pepper
1/2 tsp onion powder
1/2 tsp garlic powder
1/4 tsp fresh garlic
2 tbsp soy sauce
1 tsp kosher salt
4 rustic ciabatta buns

Mix the meat well. Divide into four 1/2 lb burgers. Shape and refrigerate. Take out a few minutes before grilling.

Spicy Mayonnaise

1/2 cup mayonnaise
2 fried jalapeños
1 tsp kosher salt
1 tsp dry thyme
1 tsp onion powder
1 tsp ground garlic
1 tsp freshly ground black pepper, plus additional for seasoning
pinch cayenne pepper
2 tbsp non-dairy sour cream
1 tsp lemon juice
1 tsp paprika

Place all the ingredients in a food processor and blend 1-2 minutes until smooth.

Preheat grill. Grill beef steak burgers until medium. Heat pulled beef. Toast buns and spread with spicy mayonnaise on both sides. Place burger on bun, add pulled beef and top with pastrami. Cover with top bun.

Savor the Flavor & Enjoy!

Fish & Vegetarian

Blackened Red Snapper with Dijon Mustard Dipping Sauce

Serves 4

4 (6 oz) red snapper fillets
2 tbsp Cajun spread
4 tbsp Cajun mix
2 tbsp olive oil

In a small bowl, mix Cajun mix with olive oil. Dip snapper and rub well.

Heat a large iron skillet over high heat until extremely hot.

Add Cajun spread. Place fish fillets in hot skillet. Cook until coating on fillet turns black, 3-5 minutes. Turn fish and repeat on other side. Fish will be very dark.

Let sit for 2-4 minutes until fish begins to flake.

Dijon Mustard Dipping Sauce with Capers

1/4 cup Dijon mustard
1/2 tsp fresh ground pepper very coarse
1 tbsp mayonnaise
1 tsp mustard seeds
1 tsp fresh dill
1 tsp capers with juice
a pinch of cayenne pepper

Mix all ingredients, blending well.

Aunt Bobbie's Salmon in a Bag

Serves 6

6 (6-8 oz) salmon fillets, skin on
1/4 cup fresh tarragon
2 tsp ground garlic
2 tbsp lemon juice
2 tsp kosher salt
1/2 tsp white pepper
2 tsp mustard seeds
3/4 cup shelled pumpkin seeds toasted
1/2 cup cilantro leaves
1/2 cup extra-virgin olive oil
2 lemons washed and sliced thin
1 onion peeled and sliced

Preheat oven or gas grill to 400°F.

In a food processor add 1/3 cup of the toasted pumpkin seeds, mustard seeds, white pepper, cilantro, tarragon, garlic and process until chopped well. Add lemon juice and oil slowly, creating a pesto-like purée. Add the salt and pepper to taste.

Preheat a skillet and add 2 tbsp of olive oil. Sear the salmon skin side down for 2-3 minutes. Remove from pan and put aside to cool.

Pour pesto purée over salmon with skin side up. Make foil or parchment envelope for the salmon. You will need 6 of these. On each sheet place 2 slices of lemon and 2 slices of onion to create a bed for the salmon. Place the salmon over lemon and onion. Pour some extra purée over salmon and fold edges. Repeat for the other 5 pieces. Place in oven for 12-16 minutes.

Open with care since there will be steam. Add some of the toasted pumpkin seeds on top of salmon and serve.

Grilled Red Snapper with Watermelon and Jalapeño Salsa

Serves 6

6 (5-6 oz) red snapper fillets
1 tsp onion powder
1 tsp garlic powder
1 tsp paprika
1 tsp freshly ground pepper
1 tsp kosher salt
4-5 tbsp extra virgin olive oil
2 cups chopped seedless watermelon
1/2 cup yellow bell peppers diced small
1 small jalapeño pepper, seeded and minced
1 tsp fresh chopped thyme
2 tbsp fresh chopped Italian parsley
2 tbsp minced red onion
2 tbsp aged balsamic vinegar

Preheat your grill or non-stick skillet.

In a bowl, mix onion powder, garlic powder, salt, pepper and 3 tbsp of olive oil. Rub over the snapper. Let sit for a few minutes.

While snapper is marinating, make the salsa.

Mix chopped watermelon, yellow peppers, jalapeño, thyme, parsley, onions and vinegar with olive oil. Allow the flavors to blend.

To grill snapper, use non-stick spray for grill or skillet. Grill on both sides for 3-4 minutes. Plate and serve with salsa on top.

Nir's Tip: Though not Kosher, a great addition to the salsa is feta cheese. Cut feta to the same size cubes as the watermelon.

Southern Fried Smelt

18 - 20 smelts
1 egg beaten
1 bottle of beer (12 oz)
1 cup all purpose flour
1 tsp kosher salt
1/2 tsp sweet paprika
oil for frying

Clean smelts and wash thoroughly then wipe dry. Fill a heavy pan or iron skillet 1/3 full. Heat oil over a medium to high heat. Don't go over 375°F. Use the thermometer if necessary.

Mix egg with beer, add flour, salt, sweet paprika and mix until batter is smooth. Dip smelt in batter and fry until crisp and golden brown, 3-4 minutes on each side. Fry 4-6 fish at a time. Remove from oil and drain on absorbent paper

This dish is best from pan to table.

Nir's Tip: Sprinkle with fresh chopped flat parsley, lemon juice and southern hot sauce or blend Cajun mix into the batter.

Smelts
in your mouth,
fries in a pan

Fried Sand Dabs with Lemon Aioli

Serves 6 - 8

2 lbs sand dabs
4 eggs beaten
1/4 cup soy or almond milk
1/2 cup flour seasoned with 1 tsp salt and 1/2 tsp pepper
1/4 cup chopped Italian parsley
1/2 cup panko bread crumbs
1/2 tsp of Cajun mix
1/4 cup canola oil

In a bowl, beat soy/almond milk and eggs. Add chopped parsley. Preheat heavy iron skillet and add oil, making sure there is enough oil for frying. Add salt and pepper to the flour. Dredge sand dabs in flour then dip in egg mixture. Remove from egg mixture and dip in panko. Press well on both sides and put in hot oil.   Cook for 3-4 minute each side until brown.

Remove and place on a tray lined with paper towel.

Lemon Aioli

1/2 cup mayonnaise
1 tsp finely grated lemon zest
2 tbsp fresh lemon juice
1 tbsp tsp Dijon mustard
2 whole sautéed garlic cloves
1/2 tsp kosher salt
1/2 tsp ground pepper
1 tbsp chopped chives
1 tbsp canola oil

In a preheated skillet, add oil and on a medium heat, sauté whole garlic until golden light brown. Remove from oil and let sit.

In a food processor, mix mayonnaise and lemon zest. Add lemon juice, Dijon mustard, garlic and oil from garlic. Add salt and pepper to taste. Put in a mixing bowl and add chopped chives.

Aunt Vennie's Kale and Red Pepper Quiche

Serves 6 - 8

1 sheet puff pastry dough 10 x 14
2 tbsp margarine
2 tbsp bread crumbs
2 large shallots sliced thin
5 fresh eggs
1/2 cup soy or almond milk
4 tbsp flour
2 tsp thyme
1 cup non dairy cream cheese
1/3 cup non dairy sour cream
1/3 cup non dairy shredded chedder cheese
2 tbsp olive oil
3 cups small kale, sliced very thin
2 sweet red peppers, seeded and chopped
1 tsp kosher salt
1 tsp white pepper
1/2 tsp nutmeg (fresh ground)

Preheat oven to 375°F.

Grease a 9 x 13 pan with margarine. Place puff pastry dough on a clean work area and roll out with a rolling pin. Sprinkle bottom of baking pan with bread crumbs. Line 9 x 13 pan with puff pastry dough. Press dough into pan and pierce with fork. This will prevent the dough from puffing up.

Bake in oven for 10 minutes or until the dough forms a light golden color. Sauté the kale, shallots and red peppers for 3-4 minutes. Remove from pan and let cool.

In a large mixing bowl, add eggs, soy milk, flour, cheese, cream cheese, salt, pepper and fresh nutmeg. Whisk well. Make sure the cream cheese mixes well. Add kale, peppers and shallots. Pour into baked shell. Let sit for 1 minute. Lift and pound once or twice on counter to remove any air from mix.

Place on middle rack of oven and bake for 40-45 minutes. The center should be dry after 40 minutes.

The French may have created Quiche *but this definitely has* a Soul Food Niche!

Desserts & Breads

Chocolate Pecan Brownie

Serves 8 - 10

6 oz unsalted margarine at room temperature
4 oz dark chocolate, chopped
4 large eggs
1 cup granulated sugar (if using bitter-sweet dark chocolate add 3/4 cup sugar)
1 1/2 tsp pure vanilla extract
1/4 tsp kosher salt
3 cups plus 3/4 cup all purpose flour
1/4 cup cocoa powder
1 1/2 cups coarsely chopped pecans

Preheat the oven to 350°F.

Grease a 9 x 13 inch pan.

Melt margarine and chocolate in a saucepan on a low heat. Stir constantly until melted and smooth. Remove from the heat and set aside.

In a mixing bowl, whisk eggs. Gradually add sugar whisking until well blended. While mixing, add chocolate/margarine mixture, vanilla extract and salt. Once well mixed, add flour, cocoa, and pecans.

With a rubber spatula, pour batter in well-greased pan. Make sure batter is even. Bake for 20-25 minutes. Insert a thin knife or toothpick. Depending on how soft you want your brownie, there should be some soft crumbs and chocolate sticking to your utensil. If you like brownies dry, make sure knife comes out dry.

Let cool and cut into squares.

Nir's Tip : Garnish brownies with marshmallows. You can toast or torch them to give them a softer texture.

Pound Cake

Serves 6 - 8

1/2 lb unsalted margarine (2 sticks) at room temperature plus extra for greasing pan
3 large eggs
3 egg yolks
2 tsp pure vanilla extract
1 3/4 cups cake flour, plus extra for dusting pan
1/2 tsp kosher salt
1 1/4 cups sugar

In a small bowl, whip eggs, egg yolks and vanilla until well blended. Let egg mixture stand at room temperature until ready to use.

Generously butter 9 x 5 inch loaf pan. Dust pan with flour and knock out any excess.

In a mixer blend margarine and salt at medium-high speed until creamy, scraping the bottom and sides of bowl with a rubber spatula. Reduce speed and gradually pour in sugar. Once all sugar is added, increase speed to medium-high and beat until mixture is fluffy. With mixer running, gradually add egg mixture in slow, steady stream, scraping bottom and sides of bowl. Beat mixture at medium-high speed until light and fluffy.

Remove bowl from mixer and scrape bottom and sides.

Sift flour over egg mixture, folding gently with rubber spatula until combined. Scrape along bottom of bowl and sides.

Transfer batter to loaf pan and smooth surface with rubber spatula.

Bake 65-70 minutes until golden brown. Insert a knife or wooden skewer into center of cake and if it comes out clean, cake should be done. Cool cake in pan on wire rack.

Pecan Pie

Serves 6 - 8

1 cup light or dark corn syrup
3 eggs
1 cup sugar
2 tbsp margarine, melted
1 tsp pure vanilla extract
1 1/2 cups pecans
1 unbaked pie crust (9 inch)

Sweet and Savory Pie Crust

1 3/4 cups all-purpose flour
1 tsp of kosher salt
1 stick plus 2 tbsp cold unsalted margarine, cut into cubes
1/3 cup ice water

In a food processor, pulse flour with salt. Add margarine cubes and pulse until coarsely mixed. Add ice water and pulse until dough starts to come together. Scrape dough out of mixer onto a clean work surface. Roll dough into a ball and wrap with plastic wrap. Refrigerate until well-chilled, 1 hour or for up to 2 days.

Roll out and place in desired pie pan.

Preheat oven to 350°F.

Mix corn syrup, eggs, sugar, margarine and vanilla. Stir in pecans. Pour filling into raw pie crust.

Bake on center rack of oven for 60-70 minutes. Cool before serving.

Cinnamon Raisin and Vanilla Bean Bread Pudding

Serves 8

1 lb challah or egg bread, cubed
1 tsp cinnamon
1/2 cup egg mixed
4 egg whites
1/3 cup sugar
2 cups almond milk
2 cups whipped topping
2 tsp vanilla extract
1 vanilla bean, scraped
1/3 cup raisins
3 tbsp powdered sugar

Preheat oven to 350°F.

Spray 8 baking bowls with cooking spray and set aside.

Cut challah bread into large cubes. Toast in oven until golden.

Place bread cubes in large bowl and sprinkle with cinnamon. In a medium bowl, whisk eggs, egg whites, sugar, almond milk, whipped topping, vanilla beans and vanilla extract until blended.

Pour over bread, sprinkle with raisins and mix. Pour mixture into prepared baking bowls.

Bake 45 minutes in preheated oven or until top is puffed and golden.

Sprinkle with powdered sugar and serve.

Nir's Tip: Goes great with vanilla ice cream.

Grandma Eva's Peach Cobbler

Serves 6

6 small soufflé dishes or ramekins (3" - 4")
12 fresh medium size peaches, sliced into eighths
4 tbsp sugar
3 tbsp whiskey
3 whole eggs
1 cup sugar
1 cup soft unsalted margarine
1 1/2 cups flour

Preheat oven to 350°F.

Sprinkle peaches with whiskey, 2 tbsp of the sugar and let sit for 60 minutes.

With an electric mixer, whip eggs, remaining sugar and margarine on high for 5 minutes.

Mix in flour slowly and beat on low for 3-5 minutes.

Pour batter into 6 well greased ramekins or soufflé dishes. Place peaches on the batter pushing them halfway into batter. Pour juice from peaches, whiskey and sugar mixture evenly on the 6 portions.

Place in oven and bake 25 minutes or until golden. Stick a toothpick into the batter, if it comes out dry, your dessert is ready. Let sit for 10 minutes, then serve hot.

Pumpkin Pie

Serves 6 - 8

1 can (16 oz) pumpkin pie filling
1 cup whipped topping
2 large eggs
1 tsp ground cinnamon
1/2 tsp ground ginger
1/2 tsp ground nutmeg
1/2 tsp kosher salt
1 unbaked pie crust (9 inch)

Sweet and Savory Pie Crust

1 3/4 cups all-purpose flour
1 tsp of kosher salt
1 stick plus 2 tbsp cold unsalted margarine, cut into cubes
1/3 cup ice water

In a food processor, pulse flour with salt. Add margarine cubes and pulse until coarsely mixed. Add ice water and pulse until dough starts to come together. Scrape dough out of mixer onto a clean work surface. Roll dough into a ball and wrap with plastic wrap. Refrigerate until well-chilled for 1 hour. Roll out and place in desired pie pan.

Preheat oven to 375°F.

Whisk pumpkin mix, whipped topping, eggs, spices and salt in medium bowl until smooth. Pour mixture into crust and bake for 50 minutes or until skewer inserted into cake comes out dry. Remove from oven and let cool. Garnish with whipped cream and serve.

Whipped Sweet Potato Pie with Marshmallow Meringue

Serves 6 - 8

1 lb sweet potatoes
1/2 cup unsalted margarine
1 cup white sugar
1/2 cup almond milk
2 eggs
1/2 tsp nutmeg
1/2 tsp cinnamon
1 tsp pure vanilla extract
1 unbaked pie crust (9 inch)

Sweet and Savory Pie Crust

1 3/4 cups all-purpose flour
1 tsp of kosher salt
1 stick plus 2 tbsp cold unsalted margarine, cut into cubes
1/3 cup ice water

In a food processor, pulse flour with salt. Add margarine cubes and pulse until coarsely mixed. Add ice water and pulse until dough starts to come together. Scrape dough out of mixer onto a clean work surface. Roll dough into a ball and wrap with plastic wrap. Refrigerate until well-chilled, 1 hour or for up to 2 days. Roll out and place in desired pie pan.

Preheat oven to 350°F.

In a small pot, boil sweet potatoes whole in skin until tender. Cool and remove skin. Add sweet potatoes to food processor. Add margarine and blend well. Add sugar, almond milk, eggs, nutmeg, cinnamon and vanilla. Mix on medium speed until smooth. Pour filling into unbaked pie crust.

Bake for 60 minutes or until knife inserted in center comes out clean. Pie will puff up like a soufflé and will sink down as it cools.

Marshmallow Meringue

3 egg whites
1/2 tsp pure vanilla extract
1/8 tsp kosher salt
1/4 cup sugar
1 jar (7 oz) marshmallow cream

Raise temperature of oven to 400°F or you can use a pastry torch for this.

Beat egg whites, vanilla extract and salt at high speed until foamy, gradually adding sugar, 1 tbsp at a time. Beat until stiff peaks form.

Beat marshmallow cream into egg white mixture in 4 parts, beating until smooth. Spread over pie.

Place in oven at 400 °F for 5-6 minutes for a nice roasted color on marshmallow.

Strawberry Shortcake

Serves 6

3 cups strawberries, stemmed and quartered
5 tbsp sugar
2 cups all-purpose flour
2 tsp baking powder
1/4 tsp baking soda
2 cups sugar
3/4 tsp kosher salt
2 cups whipped cream

Whipped Cream

2 cups whipped topping
3 tbsp sugar
1/2 tsp vanilla extract
1 tsp freshly grated lemon zest

Mix strawberries with 3 tbsp sugar and refrigerate for 1 hour while berries soak in water.

Preheat the oven to 375°F.

Sift together flour, baking powder, baking soda, remaining 2 tbsp. sugar and salt in a medium bowl. Add whipped topping and mix. Place mixture in an ungreased 8-inch square pan, and bake 20-25 minutes until golden brown or until skewer inserted into cake comes out dry. Remove shortcake from pan and place on a rack to cool slightly. Cut into 6 pieces and split each piece in half horizontally.

Using a mixer blend the whipped topping, sugar, vanilla, and lemon zest until soft peaks form. Take some of the whipped topping and mix it into the strawberry mixture and fold gently with a rubber spatula. The cream will get a nice pink color from the juices.

Layer strawberries, whipped cream and shortcake. Top with strawberries and whipped cream.

Sweet Jalapeño Challah

Serves 6 - 8

1 packet active dry yeast
2/3 cup warm water
1/3 cup sugar
1/3 cup extra virgin olive oil plus more for the bowl
3 eggs, divided (2 for the bread, one for the egg wash)
1 1/2 tsp kosher salt
4 cups all-purpose flour, plus more for kneading
1/4 cup sliced jalapeño
1/4 cup chopped coarse jalapeño

Preheat the oven to 375°F.

In a large bowl, mix yeast and sugar in 1/3 cup warm water. Let mixture sit for 10 minutes so the yeast can activate. It will become foamy.

Add remaining sugar, olive oil, 2 of the eggs, salt and chopped jalapeño. Continue mixing until completely blended. Slowly add flour, stirring well.

On a clean workspace, sprinkle a little flour. Remove dough from mixer to workspace.

Knead the dough by hand for 8-10 minutes and add the chopped peaches. Knead dough until smooth. Form the dough into a large ball.

In a large bowl, add 2 tbsp olive oil and dough. Turn dough to make sure it is completely covered with oil. Cover bowl and place in a warm area.

Let the dough rise for about an hour. It should double in size.

Divide the dough into 2 or 3 long pieces so it can be braided. Transfer the braided challah to a well-floured baking sheet.

Place jalapeños on the top of the challah and press down. In a small bowl, mix one egg with 2-4 tbsp water to make an egg wash. With a pastry brush, brush the dough with the egg wash and return warm area. Let the challah rise for another 30-45 minutes

Once ready to be placed in oven, brush again with egg wash. Bake 30-40 minutes.

Peach Challah

Serves 6 - 8

1 packet active dry yeast
2/3 cup warm water
1/3 cup sugar
1/3 cup extra virgin olive oil plus more for the bowl
3 eggs (2 for the bread, one for the egg wash)
1/2 tsp kosher salt
4 cups all-purpose flour, plus more for kneading
1 cup chopped large peaches
1 cup sliced peaches

Preheat the oven to 375°F.

In a large bowl, mix yeast and sugar in 1/3 cup warm water. Let mixture sit for 10 minutes so the yeast can activate. It will become foamy. Add remaining sugar, olive oil, 2 of the eggs and salt. Continue mixing until completely blended. Slowly add flour, stirring well.

On a clean workspace, sprinkle a little flour. Remove dough from mixer to workspace. Knead the dough by hand for 8-10 minutes and add the chopped peaches. Knead dough until smooth. Form dough into a large ball.

In a large bowl, add 2 tbsp olive oil and dough. Roll dough around to make sure it is completely covered with oil. Cover bowl and place in a warm area.. Let the dough rise for 1 hour or until doubled in size.

Divide the dough into 2 or 3 long pieces so it can be braided. Transfer the braided challah to a well floured baking sheet. Place 1 cup of sliced peaches on the top of the challah and press down.

In a small bowl, mix one egg with 2-4 tbsp water to make an egg wash. With a pastry brush, brush the dough with the egg wash and return warm area. Let the challah rise for 30-45 minutes.

Brush again with egg wash and bake 30-40 minutes.

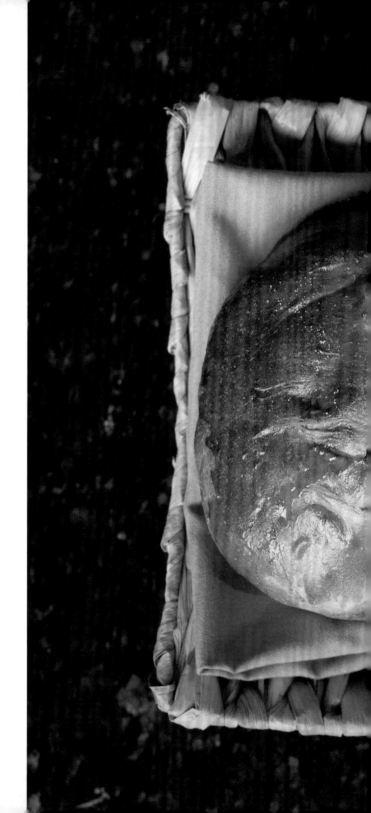

Tere's Challah With Olives

Serves 6 - 8

1 packet active dry yeast
2/3 cup warm water
1/3 cup extra virgin olive oil plus more for the bowl
3 eggs, divided (2 for bread, one for egg wash)
1/2 tsp kosher salt
4 cups all-purpose flour, plus more for kneading
sesame and/or poppy seeds
1 cup sliced kalamata olives or dried Moroccan olives

Preheat the oven to 375°F.

In a large bowl, mix yeast in 2/3 cup warm water, and let sit for 10 minutes so yeast can activate. It will become a foamy mixture. Add olive oil, 2 of the eggs and salt. Continue mixing until completely blended. Slowly add flour, stirring well.

On a clean workspace, sprinkle a little flour. Remove dough from mixer to workspace. Knead dough by hand for 8-10 minutes and add olives. Knead until smooth. Form dough into a large ball.

In a large bowl, add 2 tbsp olive oil and dough. Roll dough around to make sure it is completely covered with oil. Cover bowl and place in a warm area.

Let the dough rise for about an hour. It should double in size. Divide the dough into 2 or 3 long pieces so it can be braided. Transfer the braided challah to a well floured baking sheet.

In a small bowl, mix one egg with 2-4 tbsp water to make an egg wash. With a pastry brush, brush the dough with the egg wash and return warm area. Let the challah rise for 30-45 minutes.

Once ready to be placed in oven, brush again with egg wash and sprinkle with chopped olives, sesame and/or poppy seeds. Bake 30-40 minutes or until golden-brown.

Cornbread

Serves 6 - 8

1/2 cup margarine
2/3 cup white sugar
2 eggs
1 cup soy or almond milk
1/2 tsp baking soda
1 cup cornmeal
1 cup all-purpose flour
1/2 tsp kosher salt

Preheat oven to 375°F.

Grease an 8 inch square pan. Melt margarine in large skillet. Remove from heat and stir in sugar. Quickly add eggs and beat until well blended. Combine soy or almond milk with baking soda and stir into mixture in pan. Stir in cornmeal, flour, and salt until well blended and few lumps remain. Pour batter into the prepared pan.

Bake for 30 to 40 minutes, or until a toothpick inserted in the center comes out clean.

Lady Meshuguna!

Drinks

Sweet Red Wine and Fruit Cooler

Serves 8 - 10

2 bottles red wine
1 cup brandy
1/2 cup triple sec
1 cup orange juice
1 cup pomegranate juice
1/2 cup simple syrup
orange slices
apple slices
blackberries
pomegranate seeds

To prepare simple syrup, mix 1/2 cup of granulated sugar
and 1/2 cup of distilled water in a small saucepan. Heat to
dissolve sugar, stirring constantly. Set aside to cool.

Mix all ingredients together in a pitcher. Mix lightly and let
stand for at least 24 hours in a refrigerator before serving.

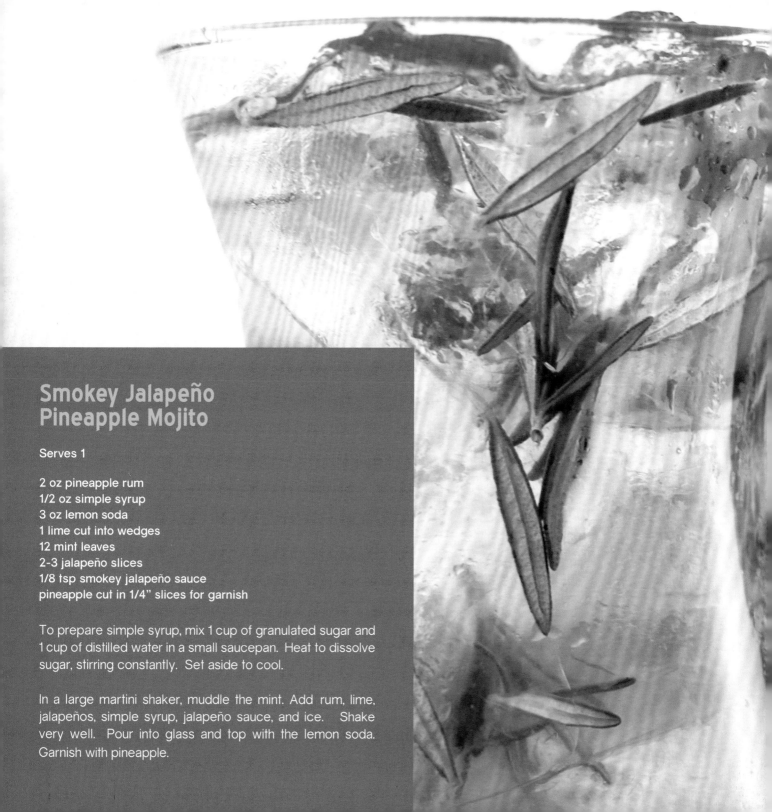

Smokey Jalapeño Pineapple Mojito

Serves 1

2 oz pineapple rum
1/2 oz simple syrup
3 oz lemon soda
1 lime cut into wedges
12 mint leaves
2-3 jalapeño slices
1/8 tsp smokey jalapeño sauce
pineapple cut in 1/4" slices for garnish

To prepare simple syrup, mix 1 cup of granulated sugar and 1 cup of distilled water in a small saucepan. Heat to dissolve sugar, stirring constantly. Set aside to cool.

In a large martini shaker, muddle the mint. Add rum, lime, jalapeños, simple syrup, jalapeño sauce, and ice. Shake very well. Pour into glass and top with the lemon soda. Garnish with pineapple.

Mint Julep

Serves 8

4 cups bourbon
2 bunches fresh mint
1 cup simple syrup

To prepare simple syrup, mix 1 cup of granulated sugar and 1 cup of distilled water in a small saucepan. Heat to dissolve sugar, stirring constantly. Set aside to cool.

Pour 4 cups of bourbon into a glass pitcher. Add 1 cup simple syrup to the bourbon and stir. Refrigerate.

To serve the julep, fill each glass half-full with shaved ice. Crush a spring of mint to release flavor and add to glass. Top with more shaved ice.

When frost forms on the cup, pour refrigerated julep mixture over the ice. Serve immediately.

Fresh Lemonade

Serves 4 - 6

6 lemons
1 cup simple syrup
5 cups cold water

To prepare simple syrup, mix 1 cup of granulated sugar and 1 cup of distilled water in a small saucepan. Heat to dissolve sugar, stirring constantly. Set aside to cool.

Juice the lemons to make 1 cup of juice. In a large pitcher combine 1 cup lemon juice, 1 cup simple syrup and 5 cups cold water. Stir. Adjust water to taste. Chill and serve over ice.

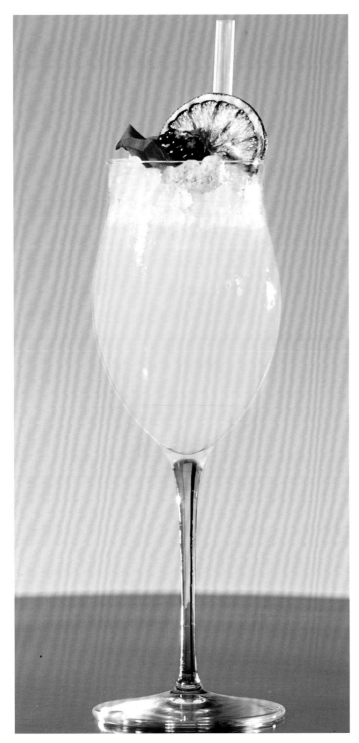

Mango Spritzer

Serves 6

ice cubes
4 cups mango juice
4 cups sparkling wine or sparkling grape juice
1/2 cup fresh lime juice
8 lime slices

Chill wine and juices. In pitcher combine the mango juice, sparkling wine or seltzer and lime juice. Stir well.

Fill 6 glasses with ice and add spritzer. Garnish with the lime slices and serve.

Blended Mint Lemonade

Serves 3 - 4

1/2 cup simple syrup
1/2 cup fresh lemon juice
4 cups water
1 bunch mint leaves
18-20 ice cubes

To prepare simple syrup, mix 1 cup of granulated sugar and 1 cup of distilled water in a small saucepan. Heat to dissolve sugar, stirring constantly. Set aside to cool.

Add simple syrup, 4 cups of water, lemon juice, mint leaves and ice cubes to a blender. Blend until drink has a smooth consistency.

Pour into tall glasses and garnish with mint leaves.

Ginger Peach Punch

Serves 4 - 6

3 family-size tea bags
1 (33 oz.) bottle peach nectar
1 1/2 cups fresh lemon juice
1/2 cup simple syrup
1 liter bottle ginger ale, chilled
1 liter bottle club soda, chilled
fresh peach wedges for garnish

To prepare simple syrup, mix 1 cup of granulated sugar and 1 cup of distilled water in a small saucepan. Heat to dissolve sugar, stirring constantly. Set aside to cool.

Bring 4 cups of water to a boil in a medium saucepan, add tea bags. Boil for 1 minute and remove from stove. Cover and steep for 10 minutes.

In a gallon pitcher add tea, peach nectar, fresh lemon juice and simple syrup. Cover and chill.

Pour chilled tea mixture into a punch bowl or pitcher. Stir in ginger ale and club soda just before serving. Garnish with peach wedges.

Sun Tea

Serves 4 - 6

6 tea bags
2 qts water

Place the 6 tea bags into a 2 qt glass Mason jar filled with water and cover. Place the Mason jar outside in sunlight for 4 - 6 hours.

When tea has reached its desired strength, discard tea bags and refrigerate.

Southern Hospitality Iced Tea

Serves 4 - 6

3 family-size tea bags
3 tbsp crushed fresh mint leaves
1 qt boiling water
2 cups white sugar
2 qt cold water
1 1/2 cups fresh lemon juice

Bring 4 cups water to a boil in a medium saucepan, add tea bags. Boil for 1 minute and remove from stove. Cover and steep for 10 minutes.

In a gallon pitcher, combine mint leaves with tea, lemon juice and sugar. Stir to dissolve sugar. Stir in the cold water and let cool.

Serve in tall glasses over ice. Garnish with mint leaves.

Georgia On The Porch

Serves 4

2 cups peach vodka
1 cup white grape juice
1/2 cup orange juice
1/3 cup simple syrup
1 liter bottle ginger ale, chilled

To prepare simple syrup, mix 1 cup of granulated sugar and 1 cup of distilled water in a small saucepan. Heat to dissolve sugar, stirring constantly. Set aside to cool.

Combine ingredients in glass pitcher and stir gently. Pour into glass tumblers filled with cubes of ice. Garnish with white grapes.

The Silent Partner Martini "a la George"

Serves 1

4 oz vodka, chilled
1/2 oz dry vermouth
2 bleu cheese stuffed olives

With a demi spoon stuff pitted jumbo olives with the bleu cheese.

Pour chilled vodka into martini shaker. Add dry vermouth and stir softly–do not shake. Pour contents into martini glass. Add 2 stuffed bleu cheese olives.

Charleston Old Fashioned

Serves 1

3 oz bourbon
1 orange slice
1 tsp bitters
1 tsp sugar
1/4 tsp fresh ginger
2 oz soda water

Place orange slice, bitters, sugar, and ginger in martini shaker and crush with pestle or spoon until thoroughly mixed.

Strain and pour into glass tumbler filled with ice. Add bourbon and soda water. Garnish with orange and / or lemon.

Bulldog Bloody Mary

Serves 1

1 1/2 oz pepper vodka
4 oz tomato juice
3 dashes of Worcestershire sauce
3 dashes of Green Tabasco sauce
1 tsp horseradish
1/2 oz lime juice
1/2 tsp pepper
1 tsp kosher salt
1 celery stick
1 tsp pickled okra juice
1 piece of crispy pastrami
1 wedge of lime

Mix all ingredients in a martini shaker and shake well. Pour into glass over ice. Garnish with the celery, lime, and piece of crispy pastrami.

Savannah Sangria

Serves 6

1 bottle dry red wine
1 1/2 cup of white rum
1 peach
1 cup of peach nectar
1 orange
1 lime
1 cup sugar

Be sure all ingredients (except sugar) are well chilled. Combine wine, rum, peach, orange, lime and sugar in large glass pitcher and refrigerate for 2-3 hours.

When ready to serve, crush fruit at bottom of pitcher with a wooden spoon. Add peach nectar. Pour over ice into glass rimmed with rock sugar and garnish with peach leaves.

I'm already Married so I "can't elope!"

You say Goodbye, I say, "Shalom"

Eva Mae Brown

Sandra, Harold & Sunda Croonquist

Index

Index cont.

Index cont.

Index cont.

Our Family Recipes

_____   _____

_____   _____

_____   _____

_____   _____

_____   _____

_____   _____

_____   _____

_____   _____

_____   _____

_____   _____

_____   _____

_____   _____

Our Family Recipes